PREVENTING

child& substance ABUSE

A Parent's Guide

DISCLAIMER

None of the information provided in this manual is to be looked upon as legal advice, authority, or law. Contact the local authorities (Department of Social Services, Family Services, Department of Child Welfare, etc.) for state laws and statutes that govern what is required under the laws of your individual county and state. Please consult with local police and a local attorney to find out the requirements and the laws that govern your state. The writers of this manual are not engaged in rendering legal advice. If legal advice or other expert assistance is required, the services of a competent professional should be sought.

Adapted from material from National Institute on Drug Abuse, Prevent Child Abuse America, Children's Rights of America, American Academy of Child & Adolescent Psychiatry, U.S. Department of Health and Human Services Administration for Children and Families, National Coalition Against Pornography, Marvin J. Lemke, and Joan K. Leavitt, M.D. Compiled by Royal Rangers.™

02-2137
ISBN 0-88243-996-0

GUIDELINES FOR CHILD ABUSE PREVENTION

Child abuse is an ugly reality. A single incident of abuse—if only alleged—can devastate a child, a family, a church, and a ministry.

You might find it difficult or uncomfortable to discuss child abuse with your children. However, you have the responsibility to talk with them about this important issue.

HOW TO USE THIS BOOKLET

This booklet was written to help protect your child. It describes what the church does to keep him safe. It also has information to help you train your child to avoid abuse and to report it if he encounters it. Here's how to use it:

1. Read section 1, which describes the safeguards that the church uses to protect the children in its care. (This is information for you, the parent.)
2. Read and discuss section 2 with your child. It describes the ways your child can protect himself.
3. Read and let your child answer the questions in section 3.
4. Fill out the form on the last page and give it to the leader or teacher of your child's group at church. (Some groups will require this before your child can participate in all activities.)

Section One

The church and its children's workers use the following guidelines to protect children.

GENERAL PRINCIPLES

The following principles describe the standard for all leaders (teachers and workers). These guidelines will help ensure the safety of children in the local church. Every leader is to be a model of godliness.

First Principle: Responsibility

Each leader should demonstrate appropriate behavior during meetings and events. Others, especially young and impressionable children are observing his behavior. Likewise, he should show concern for the ethical behavior of leaders and children under his direction.

Second Principle: Ability

Each leader should strive to maintain the highest standards in his ministry. A leader's ability to train others will depend upon his desire to improve his own skills. A leader should seek the knowledge, expertise, and abilities of fellow leaders. A leader must keep up to date on information, training resources, and technical resources to assist with the training of other leaders.

Third Principle: Nurture

Caring for, training, and developing children is a tremendous responsibility. A leader should always seek what is best for the children and provide as many opportunities as possible for them to grow and participate in new experiences. Many of these opportunities will come from the leader as he models Christian behavior.

Fourth and Fifth Principles: Godliness and Equity

A leader must strive to be honest, fair, and Christlike in dealings with others. Rules and expectations must be consistent. If one day it is acceptable to yell out answers without raising hands and the next day it is not, the children will be confused and uncertain about appropriate conduct. A good leader must not have favorites, but demonstrate equal concern for all.

Sixth Principle: Respect

Each leader must respect the rights and differences of each person in the group. Children come from various ethnic, social, and religious backgrounds. The leader's Christian behavior and verbal communication of the gospel will be the means of touching their hearts. A leader will avoid inconsistencies, discriminatory practices, or prejudicial treatment.

Seventh Principle: Society

A leader is training young people to take leadership in society: the church, the community, and the nation. His influence will have long-term consequences. He should live according to the laws of the land (as long as they do not conflict with the laws of God) and seek to develop this same respect for law and concern for community in each child.

STANDARDS FOR A LEADER

Every leader needs to exhibit conduct consistent with the seven principles stated above.

- **Ethics.** He (or she) should be a model in the community, maintaining a consistent witness.
- **Competence.** He should be properly trained through leadership courses and by observing experienced leaders.
- **Expertise.** He or she is to continue the development of leadership skills.
- **Age appropriateness.** He should use language and materials that can be understood by the age group.

- **Discrimination.** He will not discriminate, as prescribed by law and the church.
- **Safety.** He is responsible to take reasonable steps to keep the children out of harm's way.
- **Misuse of position.** He will not take advantage of fellow leaders, helpers, or children to obtain (or be perceived to obtain) personal, financial, social, organizational, or political gain.
- **Multiple relationships.** He will refrain from entering into or promising a relationship with a child or adult if it appears such a relationship might impair his objectivity or ability to perform required duties, or might harm or exploit the other party.
- **Sexual integrity.** He will not use the leadership position to exploit or harass others in any sexual manner. Such behavior can result in immediate dismissal or legal action. This church does not tolerate the use of pornography. He is to avoid any materials that might be considered pornographic.
- **Supervision.** He will delegate to children and other leaders or helpers only such responsibility or authority that they can reasonably perform based on their training, education, or background.
- **Training.** He will provide training so those under his supervision will be qualified to perform their duties and responsibilities.

STANDARD PROCEDURES FOR PROTECTING CHILDREN

The following guidelines help prevent child abuse:

1. Screen leaders.
   - The church will interview all applicants who are interested in children or youth ministries.
   - Have every worker who participates in children and youth ministries (both volunteer and paid) fill out an application for such ministry.
2. Establish and implement procedures and policies on corporal punishment, discipline, and dismissal action. Such procedures and policies must be understood and followed.

3. Establish job descriptions for leaders.
4. Require two adult leaders to participate in all activities (e.g., camping, field trips). Additional leadership may be required with larger activities.
5. If a leader needs to counsel a child, this should be done in a private area but in view of another adult or other individuals. If a leader needs to take a child aside for individual help, another adult should accompany them. This is not to inhibit the leader's relationship with his students but to protect those relationships from being misunderstood.
6. Respect the dignity and sanctity of every child. Privacy in bathrooms and swimming areas, for example, must be respected. The only time a leader should infringe on a child's privacy is if that child's health or safety is in jeopardy.
7. Uphold the same leadership standards in all groups. The conduct of leaders and junior leaders in every program or function should reflect the behavior outlined in this document.
8. Secret organizations or other private groups are prohibited.
9. Keep written records of unusual behaviors and occurrences.
10. If you suspect or are aware of child abuse, immediately report it to your pastor or church board. (See "When to Report" in section 2.) These church leaders should take appropriate action.

Note: If your state considers you a mandatory reporter, informing the pastor or board does not relieve you of further reporting to authorities as required by law.

Child Abuse

RECOGNIZING CHILD ABUSE

The term *abuse* can be broadly defined as "anything that brings harm upon the individual." Therefore, under the term *abuse* there are two ways in which boys can be harmed. The first type of abuse is passive. The common description of passive abuse is the word *neglect*. Neglect is the failure of an adult to prevent harm. An example is parents failing to provide clean clothes for their child.

The second type of abuse is active. The common description of active abuse is simply the word *abuse*. This is the active and intentional harm brought upon a child by an adult. An example is a bruise produced on the child by a blow dealt by the parent.

Children depend on adults for their protection. The problem of and the solution to child abuse lies within every community, and you do not have to be an expert to prevent this social blight. This section will list facts about child abuse, how to recognize abuse, and resources to help prevent child abuse. Check with your state health services department, child abuse services, or social services agencies for additional local information.

Note: Leaders must keep the pastor informed of any suspicion of child abuse. Coordinate with him any efforts of reporting child abuse to local authorities. However, if your state considers you a mandatory reporter, informing the pastor or board does not relieve you of further reporting to authorities as required by law.

Facts About Child Abuse in the United States

- In 1998 about 3 million instances of child abuse were reported to child protective service agencies. About 1 million of these reports were substantiated. In 1999 the number dropped to 716,000 substantiated reports. The child population in 1999 was around 67 million. Therefore, 1 percent of children are abused each year.
- About one thousand children die each year due to physical abuse or neglect—that's almost three children a day.
  The average age of a child who dies from abuse is 2 1/2 years old.
- An abused child who is returned to his parents without intervention has a 35 percent chance of being seriously reinjured—almost 2 percent of such children are killed.
- About one child in five will be sexually abused by the age of eighteen.
- Over 90 percent of sex offenders are known by the victim.
- More than one-third of child sexual abuse involves children five years old or younger.
- Fifty-one percent of all reported cases in 1998 involved neglect; 25 percent involved physical abuse; 10 percent involved sexual abuse; 3 percent involved emotional abuse; 11 percent were other forms of maltreatment.

- Of the nearly 3 million reports, only 1,158 were intentionally false reports, a rate of only .04 percent.
- Of the more than seven hundred thousand known victims in 1999, 52 percent were female and 48 percent were male.
- Over 70 percent of all abusers are under the age of forty.

EMOTIONAL ABUSE

Emotional abuse is chronic negative behavior toward a child, such as belittling, humiliating, and ridiculing. Emotional neglect is the consistent failure of an adult to provide a child with appropriate support, attention, and affection. Both types of maltreatment impair the psychological growth and development of a child.

Scope of the Problem

The frequency of emotional abuse approaches that of physical abuse: about 1 million victims a year. Emotional abuse typically occurs with physical abuse; however, it may occur as the only form of maltreatment or in conjunction with other forms of abuse.

Examples of emotional abuse are when an adult chronically

- Criticizes the child for behavior that is developmentally normal
- Belittles and shames the child
- Blames the child for things over which the child has little or no control
- Uses the child as a scapegoat
- Takes little or no interest in the child or the child's activities
- Treats the child differently from other children in the household or group
- Withholds love and affection
- Restricts the child's peer relationships
- Engages in bizarre acts of torture or torment, such as locking the child in a closet
- Imposes extreme forms of punishment

Behavioral Indicators

Signs of emotional abuse may be less obvious than signs of other maltreatment. Suspect emotional abuse when a child exhibits impaired development, destructive behavior, or chronic physical complaints that cannot be explained medically or circumstantially. A child who persistently shows several of the following behavioral characteristics may be experiencing emotional abuse:

- Habit disorders, such as biting, rocking, head banging, and thumb sucking in an older child
- Poor peer relationships
- Behavioral extremes—overly compliant, demanding, withdrawn, overly aggressive
- Self-destructive behavior, obliviousness to hazards and risks
- Irrational and persistent fears, dreads, or hatreds
- Physical, mental, and emotional developmental lags
- Talk of punishment that seems excessive
- Overreaction to mistakes
- Sudden speech disorders
- Self-mutilation
- Fear of parents being contacted
- Signs of drug and alcohol abuse
- Tendency to run away
- Compulsive stealing or scavenging

NEGLECT

Neglect is the chronic failure of a parent or caretaker to provide a child under eighteen with basic needs, such as food, clothing, shelter, medical care, educational opportunity, protection, supervision.

In the United States it is estimated that the occurrence of child neglect may be five times that of physical abuse.

Characteristics of Neglect

A child who persistently shows several of the following characteristics may be experiencing neglect:

- Is significantly below normal in height and weight for the age level
- Wears inappropriate clothing for the weather, has poor hygiene (including lice, body odor, scaly skin)
- Shows signs of abandonment or inadequate supervision

- Has an untreated illness or injury
- Lacks a safe, warm, sanitary shelter
- Lacks necessary medical and dental care
- Is constantly hungry
- Is constantly tired
- Is frequently late
- Has destructive tendencies
- Has a low self-esteem
- Has no social relationships
- Has a tendency to run away
- Is often irritable
- Is listless
- Has lost skin resilience

Myths and Facts about Child Neglect

Myths	Facts
• Most poor families neglect their children.	• Poverty is not neglect. Families with limited income can provide basic care for their children through various means, such as free clinics and services.
• Children will outgrow the effects of neglect.	• Well-documented cognitive and neurological deficits in children result from neglect.
• Neglect is not as serious a problem as abuse.	• Both physical abuse and neglect pose serious problems for children.
• If a family is reported for neglect, the children are automatically removed from the home.	• Children are removed only if the conditions threaten their lives, safety, or health.

PHYSICAL ABUSE

Physical abuse is any nonaccidental injury to a child under the age of eighteen caused by a parent or caretaker. Nonaccidental injuries may include beating, shaking, burning, biting, strangling, or scalding with hot water—any of which produces bruises, welts, broken bones, scars, or internal injuries. Child abuse is rarely a single physical attack, but rather behavior repeated over time. It occurs when a parent or another person willfully or maliciously injures or causes a child to be injured, tortured, or maimed, or when unreasonable force is used upon a child. Abuse may also result from overdiscipline or overly severe punishment.

The National Center on Child Abuse and Neglect estimates that as many as one hundred thousand to two hundred thousand children are physically abused each year.

Recognizing Physical Abuse

The following physical indicators will help you to recognize physical abuse:

- Unexplained bruises and welts are the most frequent evidence. Often they are on the face, torso, buttocks, back, or thighs. Many times the contusions will reflect the shape of the object used (e.g., an electrical cord, a belt buckle) and may be in various stages of healing.
- Unexplained fractures or dislocations often involve the facial structure, the skull, and the bones around joints, and may include multiple or spiral fractures.
- Unexplained burns—often on the palms, soles, buttocks, or back—may reflect a pattern indicative of cigarette, cigar, electrical appliance, hot water, rope, or carpet burns.
- Other unexplained injuries, such as lacerations, abrasions, human bite marks, pinch marks, or hair loss (bald patches) may be found.

Behavioral Indicators

A physically abused child may exhibit several of the following types of behavior:

- Requests punishment or feels deserving of it
- Is afraid to go home and requests to stay with the leader
- Is overly shy, tends to avoid physical contact with adults, especially parents

- Displays behavioral extremes (withdrawal or aggressiveness)
- Suggests that other children should be punished harshly
- Cries excessively and/or sits and stares
- Reports injury by parents
- Gives unbelievable explanations for injuries
- Will often cling to the abuser after an incident of abuse as a means to placate the abuser
- Acts out sexually
- Makes physical gestures of suicide (e.g., makes a gun with the hand and points to the head)
- Appears passive or withdrawn
- Has school problems
- Shows signs of drug and alcohol abuse

Myths and Facts about Physical Abuse

Myths	Facts
• The majority of parents who abuse children are mentally ill.	• Less than 10 percent of abusive parents have a mental disorder.
• Physical abuse occurs only in lower socioeconomic families.	• Reports of physical abuse have been confirmed in all socioeconomic levels.
• Young children have frequent accidents that break bones.	• Many broken bones in children under the age of two are the result of intentional injury.
• A physician's opinion is needed before a report of physical abuse can be made.	• Proof of injury is not necessary to make a report.
• Only children under age sixteen can be reported as physically abused.	• Physical abuse of any child under age eighteen should be reported.
• Children who are being abused by their parents will ask for help.	• Children are usually afraid to talk about their injuries or are too young to ask for help.

Sexual Abuse

Child sexual abuse is a person's exploitation of a child or adolescent for sexual gratification. This includes behaviors such as intercourse, sodomy, oral-genital stimulation, verbal stimulation, exhibitionism, voyeurism, fondling, and involving a child in prostitution or the production of pornography.

Incest is sexual abuse that occurs within a family. The abuser may be a parent, stepparent, grandparent, sibling, or cousin.

Scope of the Problem

About eighty thousand cases of child sexual abuse are confirmed annually in the United States. It is generally accepted that these figures are significantly less than the actual occurrence of abuse. Current research indicates that 25 to 33 percent of girls and 10 to 17 percent of boys will be sexually abused by age eighteen.

Child sexual abuse may be a onetime occurrence; more typically it is an abusive relationship of one to four years.

Recognizing Sexual Abuse

Unfortunately, many children do not report their abuse, and rely on adults to be aware of specific behavioral and physical indicators. A child who persistently shows several of the following characteristics may be experiencing sexual abuse:

- Has sexual knowledge or behavior beyond the child's developmental level, or avoids anything of a sexual nature
- Manifests depression, or makes suicidal gestures
- Is a chronic runaway
- Frequently complains of symptoms—such as headaches, backaches, and stomachaches—caused by mental or emotional disturbance
- Shows signs of drug or alcohol abuse
- Avoids undressing, or wears extra layers of clothing
- Suddenly avoids certain familiar adults or places
- School performance declines

- Has sleep problems or nightmares
- Is seductive
- Makes statements that the body is dirty, or complains of something wrong with the genital area

Note: The most reliable indicator of child sexual abuse is the child's verbal disclosure.

Myths and Facts about Sexual Abuse

Myths	Facts
• Sex offenders can be easily identified because they are strangers who offer rides or candy to children.	• Over 90 percent of sex offenders are known by the abused children: family members, friends, neighbors, baby-sitters.
• Most sexual abuse victims are teenagers who can protect themselves from exploitation.	• Children of all ages are sexually abused. More than one-third of the victims are five years old or younger.
• Children often lie about being sexually abused.	• Children typically do not have the experience or vocabulary to accurately describe adult sexual activity, nor do they lie to get themselves into trouble.
• Incest offenders molest children in their own families only.	• Research indicates that up to 50 percent of incest offenders also molest children outside their families.
• Lack of physical violence in child sexual abuse means the children are willing participants.	• Verbal threats and coercion are frequently used to force children to participate. Children are unable to give informed consent to sexual activity.
• Sex offenders are severely mentally disturbed, mentally retarded, or homosexuals.	• Many sex offenders appear to be responsible and respectable citizens. They may be married and appear to function well in many areas of life.

Resources for Reducing the Risk

Churches have many resources available to them to help them protect your child. One of the best is the resource kit entitled *Reducing the Risk of Child Abuse in Your Church*. If the church from which your child received this booklet is not using a resource like this, they can order it from Gospel Publishing House.

Substance Abuse

THE ROLE OF PREVENTION

Educating young people about the hazards of alcohol and other drug use and arming them with skills that discourage drug use are important components of the nation's war against drugs. To combat drug use, the entire community must be involved—parents, schools, law enforcement personnel, churches, community organizations, and, of course, young people. Each group must unite behind the consistent message that illegal drug use is harmful and wrong.

Although the use of some drugs by school-age children has declined recently, drug use continues at unacceptably high levels among junior high and high school students. In some communities, crack cocaine has drawn children into the world of drug dealing and drug use. The nation faces an unprecedented assault by new drugs as well as new versions of old drugs that are significantly more powerful than those available ten to fifteen years ago. These drugs are affecting all segments of society.

Those at Greatest Risk of Abuse

In the past boys were more likely than girls to abuse drugs or alcohol, but now boys and girls are equally at risk. The young, especially teenagers, who are at greatest risk of abusing drugs or alcohol include those

- With a family history of drug or alcohol abuse
- Who are depressed
- Who have low self-esteem
- Who feel left out or don't fit in

Facts about Alcohol and Other Drugs

Young people in grades seven through twelve face a much greater exposure to drugs than they did in earlier grades. Between the ages of thirteen and eighteen, young people are exposed to alcohol, tobacco, and drugs at school, during social activities, at part-time jobs, and through some friendships with adults. Although a young person may have made a conscious decision never to use drugs, he is still vulnerable, and the opportunities are always present.

Often young people do not feel comfortable talking with their parents about drugs, but they will confide in other trusted adults whom they perceive as nonjudgmental. Because adolescents get most of their information from peers, however, their information may be inaccurate. Children's leaders, Sunday school teachers, and other church leaders can be valuable sources of information and models of positive, healthy, responsible behavior.

In addition to needing more accurate information about drugs, young people need to make connections between drug use and its consequences for individuals and society. They need to see that drug use does not fit in with establishing and attaining productive goals in life.

DRUG USE INFORMATION

The 2000 survey conducted by the National Institute on Drug Abuse indicates that drug use has remained stable or declined in some cases. A survey was taken of eighth, tenth, and twelfth graders to determine use, availability, and perceived risk of use. The results are below.

Tobacco

- Cigarette use among teens has dropped significantly in the past decade.
- Only 14.6 percent of eighth graders had smoked in the past month compared to a high of 21 percent in 1996.
- Of twelfth graders, 31.4 percent smoked compared to 36.5 percent in 1997.

- Smokeless tobacco has also decreased among teenagers. For example, 7.6 percent of twelfth graders indicated they had used smokeless tobacco during the past month compared to 12.2 percent in 1995. Eighth and tenth graders also showed a similar decline in the use of smokeless tobacco.

ALCOHOL

- Of tenth graders, 71.4 percent reported having tried alcohol; 51.7 percent of eighth graders had tried alcohol.
- Of tenth graders, 41 percent reported having had an alcoholic drink during the previous month.
- Of tenth graders, 1.8 percent indicated daily intake.
- Of twelfth graders, 80.3 percent have tried alcohol, a number that has remained steady for the past decade.
- During the previous month, 32.3 percent of twelfth graders, 23.5 percent of tenth graders, and 8.3 percent of eighth graders reported being drunk.

MARIJUANA

- Marijuana use has increased significantly in the past decade. Nearly 50 percent of twelfth graders have tried marijuana and 6 percent indicated they use it daily.
- Of tenth graders, 19.7 percent indicated they had used marijuana in the month previous to the survey and 40.3 percent said they had tried marijuana.
- The use among eighth graders has increased from 16.7 percent in 1994 to 20.3 percent in 2000.

COCAINE

- Of tenth graders, 6.9 percent reported having tried cocaine.
- Of tenth graders, 4.4 percent reported having used cocaine during the previous month.
- The greatest increase in the use of cocaine is among twelfth graders: from 5.9 percent in 1994 to 8.6 percent in 2000.
- Of twelfth graders, 2.1 percent indicated a daily use.

INHALANTS

- Those who reported having tried inhalants (glues, gases,

sprays) were 17.9 percent of eighth graders and 16.6 percent of tenth graders.
- The greatest amount of abuse is committed by eighth graders. Some 4.5 percent indicated a daily use.

Methamphetamine

- Those who indicated they had used methamphetamine in the past year were 4.3 percent of twelfth graders, 4 percent of tenth graders, and 2.5 percent of eighth graders.
- The danger of methamphetamine is its relative ease of production. Labs can be built and used in cars, even while traveling.
- The highest concentrations of labs are located in California and in Midwest states, such as Missouri.

SIGNS OF DRUG USE

Changing patterns of performance, appearance, and behavior may signal the use of drugs. The items in the first category listed below, "Drugs and Drug Paraphernalia," are evidence of drug use. The items in the other categories may indicate drug use. Leaders should be alert to extreme changes in a child's behavior—forming a pattern associated with drug abuse. (Note: Many of these signs may also be exhibited by a child who is not using drugs but who may be having other problems at school or in the family.)

Drugs and Drug Paraphernalia

- Possession of drug-related paraphernalia: pipes, rolling papers, small decongestant bottles, small butane torches
- Possession of drugs or evidence of drugs: peculiar plants, butts, seeds, or leaves in ashtrays or clothing pockets
- Odor of drugs, incense, or other cover-up scents

Identification with the Drug Culture

- Drug-related magazines, slogans on clothing
- Conversation and jokes that are preoccupied with drugs
- Hostility in discussing drugs

Signs of Physical Deterioration

- Memory lapses, short attention span, difficulty in concentration
- Poor physical coordination, slurred or incoherent speech
- Unhealthy appearance, indifference to hygiene and grooming
- Bloodshot eyes, dilated pupils
- Lasting cough

Dramatic Changes in School Performance

- Distinct downward turn in the student's grades
- Increased absenteeism or tardiness
- Decreased interest in school
- Increased discipline problems and negative attitude

Changes in Behavior

- Chronic dishonesty (lying, stealing, cheating, trouble with police)
- Changes in friends, evasiveness in talking about new ones
- Possession of large amounts of money
- Increasing and inappropriate anger, irritability, secretiveness
- Reduced motivation, energy, self-discipline, and self-esteem
- Diminished interest in extracurricular activities and hobbies
- Association with drug-using friends
- Sudden mood changes
- Irritability and irresponsible behavior
- Withdrawal from the family

RESOURCES FOR FACTS AND OTHER INFORMATION

Many of the facts offered here were found on the web sites of the agencies listed in this section. Each year they update their facts and figures. Use of these web sites is recommended because they are often accompanied by prevention methods, detection indicators, and other links to educational and research-based web sites.

Section Two

Instructions: Read this information with your child. Have him or her answer the quiz in section 3 and then complete the form on the last page. Give the form to the leader of your child's group. Keep this booklet for future reference.

YOUTH PROTECTION

It is the responsibility of parents and adult leaders to provide a safe and caring place for you.

Below is information to help keep you safe wherever you are.

- Privacy: Adults or even children your age should never improperly touch you. Adults should ask to touch you if they wish to help you learn a new skill, for instance, when teaching you the proper stance for hitting a baseball.
- Feelings: Trust your feelings. If someone touches you and it makes you feel uncomfortable, tell that person to stop, even if you previously gave him or her permission to touch you.
- Activities: You will not be required to participate in high risk or dangerous activities without your permission or the permission of your parents.
- Secret organizations: Never allow anyone to make you join a secret organization.
- Attire: Always wear appropriate clothing, and never allow anyone to undress you.
- Discipline: Do not allow anyone to physically harm you or speak to you with anger. Say no to any inappropriate demands and requests.
- Hazing: Older children may ask you to pass a certain test to be in their group. This is *hazing*. Hazing will not be permitted at any function in this church.
- Housing: Never sleep in the same tent or cabin with older children, and never sleep alone with one adult, unless the adult is your parent or guardian.
- Showering/restrooms: Never shower or go into a restroom stall with an adult.

- Information: Do not tell strangers information they do not need.
- Gifts: Do not accept gifts from adults you or your parents do not know.

WHEN YOU FEEL THREATENED

- Be rude or unhelpful if necessary.
- Run, scream, and make a scene.
- Physically fight off any inappropriate touches or demands.
- Ask for help.

DEALING WITH ETHICAL ISSUES

Everyone should learn to deal with ethical issues that may be caused by a certain situation or person. The following will suggest the proper way to deal with such issues (see also Matthew 18:15–17).

1. In most instances where an ethical problem occurs, you will need to talk with the person you feel offended you. (This is true in all instances except where abuse has occurred or is suspected. If abuse has occurred, the abused person must report it to the appropriate authority, which may be a parent, guardian, law enforcement officer, or a child abuse hot line.)
2. If the issue cannot be resolved through the initial contact, then you or your leader should contact the department head who will then attempt to resolve the situation.
3. If the department head cannot resolve the issue, then the pastor and church board will need to help.

This code of ethics or one adopted by the local church should be administered under their authority. However, if a violation occurs during an event sponsored by an affiliated organization, action taken by those organizations may be separate from those taken by the local church. The action taken may also restrict the offender from further activity in the event.

REPORTING CHILD ABUSE

All states have laws that require reporting child abuse. If you or your parents need more information about child abuse, check with your state's department of human services, child welfare office, or social services agency.

When you report any abuse, write down the date and time you called. Write down the name of the person you spoke to on the telephone. Tell who you are, the names of your parents or guardians, and the person you believe abused you. Give his name and address if possible. Your parents will be able to help you talk to the person answering your call about what happened.

When to Report

A report should be made to proper authorities (e.g., social services) when there is reasonable cause for believing a child or adolescent has been abused. A report of suspected abuse is only a request for an investigation. The child protection service workers will investigate the report. All states protect reporters of suspected abuse from legal liability, even if the report is false, as long as the reporter does not knowingly file a false report.

If you believe abuse has occurred after your first report has been made, make another report.

What Happens to the Report

A child protection worker will investigate the reported abuse. The investigation will result in one of the following conclusions:

- Abuse or neglect ruled out
- Uncertain findings
- Abuse or neglect confirmed

Note: A report of suspected abuse is a responsible attempt to protect a child.

CHILD ABUSE PREVENTION

Treatment for victims and their families is the key to stopping abuse once it has occurred.

Since child abuse is a community problem, prevention efforts must begin at the local level. Child abuse is a knotty problem; therefore, a number of different approaches must be used.

Contact your state authorities on child abuse for information about the local programs offered in your community.

TALKING ABOUT ABUSE

Sometimes you may not want to talk about what happened, but it is important to talk with your parents. This information is for your parents (or guardians), but it is important for you to know how they can help you. Parents, remember how difficult it is for children to talk about their abuse, especially if they think it will get them into trouble. Therefore, it is important for you to handle what they tell you with sensitivity.

In talking with a child about abuse, it would be helpful if you would do the following:

- Provide a private time and place to talk.
- Do not promise that you will not tell.
- Tell him you are required by law to report the abuse.
- Do not express shock.
- As guardian do not criticize the family.
- Reassure him that he has done the right thing by telling.
- Use his vocabulary to discuss body parts, without being vulgar or using inappropriate language.
- Tell him the abuse is not his fault and he is not to blame.
- Determine his immediate need for safety.
- Let him know what will happen when you report the abuse.
- Report the abuse to the proper authorities.

Note: Many children are too young to tell about their abuse; they depend on you to notice and to report.

SUBSTANCE ABUSE PREVENTION

The problem of drug and alcohol abuse is an unfortunate part of the communities of our nation. Below, you and your parents will learn how you can resist the urge to do drugs.

- Have a strong and positive family. Parents need to be involved with their children and provide clear rules and information about the risks and dangers of drug and alcohol abuse.
- Children who succeed in school are far more likely to avoid experimenting with and becoming addicted to drugs or alcohol.

- Children involved in church are at less risk of substance abuse.
- Some church programs will teach you skills for avoiding or resisting drugs when offered, for strengthening personal attitudes, and for becoming more assertive.

What Young People Should Know about Drugs

Below is a list of things you should know in order to avoid involvement with drugs. However, most children don't learn about substance abuse, drugs, from the right people. The best source of information is through law enforcement. D.A.R.E. (Drug Abuse Resistance Education) programs and other school and law enforcement sponsored programs can provide the most current and accurate information about substance abuse. Such programs will provide you with the information to

- Know how to identify alcohol, tobacco, marijuana, cocaine, inhalants, hallucinogens, and stimulants in various forms
- Understand that the long- and short-term effects of specific drugs include addiction and death
- Understand that experimenting with drugs is using drugs
- Know how drugs are pushed and how society fights the drug-supply problem
- Know that laws about the use, manufacture, and sale of drugs are designed to protect people
- Understand addiction and know how it affects individuals and their families
- Know that tobacco in any form is unhealthy
- Understand how steroids can damage the body and mind
- Know how and why the effects of drugs vary from person to person, especially immediately after use
- Know how drugs affect different parts of the body—especially the circulatory, respiratory, nervous, and reproductive systems—and why drugs are dangerous for growing bodies and developing minds
- Know how drug use is related to certain diseases and disabilities, such as AIDS, learning disorders, physical impairments, birth defects, as well as heart, lung, and liver disease

- Understand that taking a combination of drugs, whether illegal or prescription, can be fatal
- Know that drug use can undermine opportunities for personal growth and professional success

DRUG PREVENTION EDUCATION

- You and your parents should have open and frank discussions about drugs and drug use.
- Learn life skills, such as problem solving, handling stress, maintaining healthy friendships, and communicating with a number of adults.
- Do not glamorize drug use by accepting the drug-using behavior of celebrities, such as singers, actors, and athletes.
- Realize that most people, including the majority of teenagers, do not use drugs.
- Learn to be responsible for your own life and decisions.
- Become self-confident.
- Get involved in other activities—such as camping, sports, and music—as a way to deal with stress.
- Develop worthwhile life goals, such as continuing your education and developing work skills that will enable a legal source of income.

SPECIFIC DRUGS AND THEIR EFFECTS

Tobacco

A fourth of all people in the United States smoke. In our society, smoking a tobacco product is the chief avoidable cause of death. In other words, a person can avoid dying due to tobacco use just by not using tobacco. Smokers are more likely than nonsmokers to develop heart disease. In fact, every year about 22 percent of all deaths—over four hundred thousand deaths—stem from smoking-related diseases. Lung, larynx, esophageal, bladder, pancreatic, and kidney cancers also strike smokers at higher rates than nonsmokers; for example, 87 percent of lung cancer deaths are linked to smoking. Chronic obstructive lung diseases, such as emphysema and chronic bronchitis, are ten times more likely to occur among smokers than nonsmokers.

However, those who quit can cut their risk of heart disease in half.

Cigarette smoke contains some four thousand chemicals, forty-three of which are known to cause cancer. Other toxins and irritants in smoke can irritate the eyes, nose, and throat. Another component, carbon monoxide, combines with hemoglobin in the blood stream to form carboxyhemoglobin; this stuff interferes with the body's ability to get and use oxygen. But perhaps the most dangerous ingredient in tobacco smoke is nicotine. For one thing, it is involved in the onset of heart attacks and cancer. But its most lethal role is reinforcing and strengthening the desire to smoke. Nicotine is highly addictive; that is why people find it very difficult to stop smoking.

The effects of smoking are harmful—no question. Nevertheless, simply quitting can reverse much of the damage.

Alcohol

Drinking alcohol causes many changes in a person's behavior. Even a small amount affects the ability to make proper judgments and to safely operate anything mechanical, including bicycles and cars; drinking makes accidents more likely. Alcohol can also put people in a fighting mood, leading to physical abuse. Drinking lots of alcohol can affect a person's ability to learn and remember information. It can also kill you. Taking drugs with alcohol can also kill.

Repeated use of alcohol can lead to dependence. Alcoholics who suddenly quit drinking alcohol experience withdrawal symptoms, including severe anxiety, tremors, hallucinations, convulsions, and possibly death. Drinking large quantities of alcohol on a long-term basis can permanently damage organs, such as the brain and the liver. This is particularly true when the drinker does not have a healthy diet.

Anabolic Steroids

Anabolic steroids are a group of powerful compounds closely related to the male sex hormone testosterone. Developed in the 1930s, steroids are seldom prescribed today. Acceptable medical uses are limited, but steroids can help certain kinds of anemia, severe burns, asthma, and some types of breast cancer.

Along with a program of muscle-building exercise and diet, steroids may contribute to one's weight and strength. Because of this, athletes in a variety of sports have used steroids since the 1950s. Besides athletes, increasing numbers of young people are trying to accelerate their physical development with steroids.

However, steroid users subject themselves to more than seventy side effects, ranging from liver cancer to psychological reactions. The liver and the cardiovascular and reproductive systems are seriously affected by steroid use. In males, use can cause withered testicles, sterility, and impotence. In females, irreversible masculine traits can develop along with breast reduction and sterility. Psychological effects in both sexes include depression and very aggressive behavior, termed "roid rage." While some side effects show up quickly, others, such as heart attacks and strokes, may not show up for years.

Signs of steroid use include the following:

- Quick weight and muscle gains (if steroids are being used in conjunction with a weight-training program)
- Behavioral changes, particularly increased aggressiveness
- Jaundice
- Purple or red spots on the body
- Swelling of the feet or lower legs
- Trembling
- Unexplained darkening of the skin
- Persistent unpleasant breath odor

Steroids are produced in a couple of different forms: as a tablet (or capsule) to be taken by mouth and as a liquid to be injected into the muscle.

COMPUTER AND INTERNET CONCERNS

Probably the greatest area of concern for the future is the risk you might face while on the Internet. Talk with your parents about whom you may speak to as well as what is appropriate and inappropriate for you to look at. You have learned to avoid unwanted touches or abuse from others; likewise, you need to be careful what you say to people or what information you give out while on-line or in a chat room.

Always discuss with your parents conversations or questions you have while on the computer. They will help you to make wise decisions about whom to talk to and what to say. Never, never give personal information to someone on the Internet or agree to meet.

Section Three

Read and answer the following questions. *You will need to write down the answers given by your child if he is too young to do so. If he does not understand or fails to give the correct answer, review that information with him.*

1. You give an adult permission to help you practice your base-ball swing. However, the way he is touching you makes you feel uncomfortable. What should you do?
2. A friend asks you to join a secret club. What should you do?
3. A stranger asks where you live. What should you do?
4. Write down one thing you can do if you feel threatened.
5. If you believe that someone has abused you, what should you do?
6. You tell your mom or dad that you believe someone has abused you. They tell you they will report it to the appropriate authorities. Is this correct? Circle YES or NO.
7. Someone offers you something that looks like it might be a drug. What should you do?
8. A friend says that he can get some steroids to help make your body bigger and stronger. What should you do?

You will need to keep this book at home. You may need it later. The last page should be filled out by one of your parents, and you will need to sign it.

Answers to Quiz

1. Tell him to stop and tell another adult (parent).
2. Tell him NO and tell an adult or parent.
3. Tell him NO and run away and scream.
4. Be rude or unhelpful. Run, scream, and make a scene. Physically fight off any inappropriate touch or demand. Ask for help.
5. Tell an appropriate adult (for example, a parent or police officer).
6. YES.
7. Tell him NO and tell an adult.
8. Tell him NO and tell an adult.

I, _____, hereby confirm that I have read section 1 detailing how the church and the home can provide a safe and caring environment for my child, _____.

I also hereby confirm that I have read section 2 with my child, telling him of his right to be protected and how to avoid being abused.

Lastly, I affirm that my child has read and answered the questions in section 3. I understand that he needed to answer all the questions correctly and that I was supposed to help him if he didn't.

I also understand that if I have any questions about the care of my child at church I should ask his leader and follow the procedures detailed in this booklet.

Signature of Parent/Date

Signature of Child/Date

FOR OFFICIAL USE ONLY

❏ Received   Date Received

❏ Filed   Date Filed

ISBN 0-88243-996-0

90000

9 780882 439969

GOSPEL PUBLISHING HOUSE
SPRINGFIELD, MO 65802-1894

RANGER KIDS

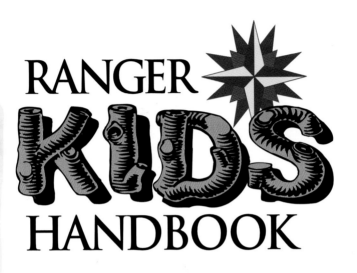

HANDBOOK

Developed by
ROYAL RANGERS®

Gospel Publishing House
Springfield, Missouri
02-2115

To churches not affiliated with the Assemblies of God: The purchase of Royal Rangers publications and resource items, such as uniforms and accessories, does not grant chartering privileges with the Royal Rangers of the General Council of the Assemblies of God. Neither does such a purchase authorize the purchaser to create or enter a Royal Rangers association with other churches or denominations. Such a purchase allows the function of the ministry within the purchasing church only.

For Ranger Kids uniforms and supplies and other Royal Rangers apparel and products, request a Royal Rangers Catalog (order number 75–2028) or a Royal Rangers order form (order number 75–2003) from Gospel Publishing House, 1445 North Boonville Avenue, Springfield, MO 65802-1894 (1-800-641-4310; there is a $5 minimum order, not applicable on free items).

Acknowledgments

Special thanks to...

Richard Mariott, for his direction and passion for the ministry of reaching, teaching, and keeping boys for Jesus Christ

Brian Hendrickson, for the compilation of this handbook

David Craun, for the chapter "Your Royal Rangers Outpost"

Stephen Graff, for the section on first aid

Ralph Glunt, for the section on being ready and safe

David Boyd, for the chapter "You and the Bible"

Fred Deaver and **Richard Mariott,** for their line art drawings and illustrations

The Ranger Kids Committee, for the years of work, planning, and ideas that were instrumental in developing the Ranger Kids program

The many individuals who helped develop and test the Advancement Trail

RANGER KIDS®

This Book Belongs to

_____
My Commander's Name

_____
My Commander's
Telephone Number

_____
My Church Is

_____
My Outpost Number Is

_____

Table of Contents

Hi Kids!

My name is J. B. Beaver, and I will be your guide as you learn about the Ranger Kids program. This is an exciting program for boys in kindergarten, first grade, and second grade. You will follow trails to activities and adventures in games, hiking, nature study, crafts, and ceremonies. Best of all, you will be guided along the trail of Bible study and Christian living. Get ready, because there are lots of exciting things ahead.

Chapter 1
Learning about Royal Rangers

Welcome to Ranger Kids.

The life of a Royal Ranger includes great indoor and outdoor adventures. You may take part in day camps, outings, and Pinewood Derbies. You will go to weekly meetings with other boys where you'll play games and make things. There will be many fun activities and events all year long. Most will be held by your outpost at your church, and some will be held by your district.

As a Royal Ranger you will grow in four ways:

1 Your body will grow strong through proper exercise and diet.

2 Your spirit will grow strong through prayer, Bible study, and witnessing.

3 Your mind will grow strong by reading, studying, and memorizing Scripture passages.

4 Your relationships with people will grow strong by learning how to treat them.

This handbook will show you how to wear the official Royal Rangers uniform. It will tell you about the Advancement Trail and how to earn the Elk Award, Wolverine Award, and Cougar Award. You will learn about many

things: your country, your community, your school, your church, your outpost, your family, and even yourself.

Royal Rangers will help you to deal with situations that you may face. You will learn to say "no" to things such as peer pressure, gangs, and drugs. And you will learn ways to say "yes" to your outpost, your church, and—most importantly—Jesus Christ.

The life of a Royal Ranger is challenging, fun, and exciting. Inside this handbook lies a trail of high adventure. So come on and join the fun. In your Ranger Kids group you will have some of the best times of your life.

A Brief History

Royal Rangers is a wonderful indoor and outdoor program that reaches thousands of boys for Christ each year. More than one million boys have taken part in Royal Rangers. They are in many nations around the world.

A little history will help you understand and enjoy the Royal Rangers ministry. This ministry to boys has been, and continues to be, done for Jesus Christ. Royal Rangers has grown because thousands of volunteers are being led and used of the Holy Spirit.

1906

God pours out His Spirit in Los Angeles, California, like He did in the Book of Acts. This starts a Movement that will go around the world. It will start many churches.

1914

The Assemblies of God begins in April in Hot Springs, Arkansas. Those who go to the meeting work out The Statement of Fundamental Truths. It defines doctrine, ethics, and goals for the new Assemblies of God.

1962

In January, Rev. Johnnie Barnes moves to Springfield, Missouri, to put together a program for boys. Rev. Charles Scott suggests the name "Royal Rangers." Rev. Barnes becomes the first Royal Rangers national commander.

1963

The Royal Rangers Leadership Training Course is developed.

1964

The first district-wide Pow Wows [now called Camps] are held. The Gold Medal of Achievement and the Medal of Valor awards are first offered.

1966

Royal Rangers programs are set up in Australia and Latin America. The Frontiersmen Camping Fraternity (later Fellowship; FCF) is formed. The first Royal Rangers Week is held. It celebrates the Royal Rangers ministry and encourages reaching, teaching, and keeping boys for Christ.

1968

National Training Camps for Royal Rangers leaders are held in four states: Missouri, Colorado, New York, and California.

1974

The first National Camporama, a camping event that happens every four years, is held at the Air Force Academy in Colorado Springs, Colorado.

1977

The National Royal Rangers Council is formed and meets in Springfield, Missouri.

11

1986

The National Royal Rangers Training Center [now National Royal Rangers Center] at Eagle Rock, Missouri is dedicated. It is also called "Camp Eagle Rock."

1989

Beloved National Commander Johnnie Barnes dies. For 27 years he led the Royal Rangers, developing its ministry. Many of his plans and projects are completed. A large army of boys is following Jesus. Rev. Ken Hunt is named national commander. He guides the ministry for ten years.

1999

Rev. Richard Mariott is appointed national commander. He was the commander for the Northern California/Nevada District for ten years and the men's director for seven years. His goals are to encourage Royal Rangers and develop new programs. New people come to the national Royal Rangers office to help him do this.

Royal Rangers Emblem

The Meaning of the Emblem

Four Gold Points Four phases of a boy's development: Physical, Spiritual, Mental, Social.

Four Red Points Four cardinal doctrines of the Church: Salvation, Baptism in the Holy Spirit, Healing, Rapture.

Eight Blue Points Eight points of the Royal Ranger Code: Alert, Clean, Honest, Courageous, Loyal, Courteous, Obedient, Spiritual.

ROYAL RANGER

CODE

A Royal Ranger Is:

ALERT
He is mentally, physically, and spiritually alert.

CLEAN
He is clean in body, mind, and speech.

HONEST
He does not lie, cheat, or steal.

COURAGEOUS
He is brave in spite of danger, criticism, or threats.

LOYAL
He is faithful to his church, family, outpost, and friends.

COURTEOUS
He is polite, kind, and thoughtful.

OBEDIENT
He obeys his parents, leaders, and those in authority.

SPIRITUAL
He prays, reads the Bible, and witnesses.

RANGER KID

ROYAL RANGER

PLEDGE

*With God's help,
I will do my best
to serve God,
my church, and
my fellowman;
to live by the
Ranger Code;
to make the
Golden Rule
my daily rule.*

Reaching, Teaching, and Keeping Boys for Christ

ROYAL RANGER

MOTTO

"Ready."

MEANING OF MOTTO:
Ready for anything!
Ready to work, play, serve,
worship, live, and obey God's Word.

THE
GOLDEN RULE:

"In everything, do to others
what you would
have them do to you"
(Matthew 7:12).

15

Royal Ranger Pledge

The Royal Ranger Pledge is very important. When a Ranger gives this Pledge, he promises to do certain things. When you make a promise, you should keep it. Study the Pledge very carefully so you can understand what you are promising.

"With God's help..."

The Pledge begins by saying that we need God's help to measure up to the Pledge. We can pray every day for His help to do this.

"With God's help, I will do my best..."

The next part of the Pledge says we will do our best. We know when we are doing our best. To be a good Ranger and a good Christian, we must always do our best in whatever we do.

"With God's help, I will do my best to serve God..."

We promise to do our best to serve God. We can serve God in many ways. We serve Him by accepting Jesus as our Savior. We serve God by praying to Him each day. We serve Him by doing what is right, obeying our parents and teachers. We serve God by choosing to not do things that are wrong, or sinful. We serve Him by studying the Bible and learning more about Him. We serve God by keeping our hearts pure and clean. We serve Him by going to church and Sunday school and by telling other people about Him.

"With God's help, I will do my best to serve God, my church..."

We serve our church by going to its services. We serve by giving offerings to the church. We serve the church by inviting people to Sunday school, church, and other special church meetings. We serve our church when we listen carefully to our Sunday school teacher and pastor. We serve when we take part in Sunday school and church by singing, testifying, and praying. We serve by doing jobs that need to be done around the church, such as picking up papers, straightening chairs, and handing out bulletins.

"With God's help, I will do my best to serve God, my church, and my fellowman..."

We also promise to serve our fellowmen. "My fellowman" means anyone we have an opportunity to serve. We can serve others by being kind and good to them and by helping them when they need help. Many lonely and sad children would like to have someone

RANGER KIDS®

like you for a friend. Best of all, we can serve others by telling them about the Lord Jesus Christ and by praying for them.

"With God's help, I will do my best to serve God, my church, and my fellowman; to live by the Ranger Code..."

The Royal Rangers Code is very important. It contains the rules that Rangers live by. We study each rule carefully so we know what is expected of us as Royal Rangers. When we promise to live by this Code, it means we will do our best to follow its rules.

"With God's help, I will do my best to serve God, my church, and my fellowman; to live by the Ranger Code; to make the Golden Rule my daily rule."

The Golden Rule is "In everything, do to others what you would have them do to you" (Matthew 7:12). These are the words of Jesus. He is telling us how He wants us to treat others. We should treat other people the way we would like to be treated.

This story may help you understand the Golden Rule.

Joe and Echo Canyon

Joe and his father were riding on their ranch. As they neared a canyon, Joe's dad said, "This is called Echo Canyon. If you shout toward the canyon walls,

18

your voice will come back to you."

"All right!" said Joe. "Let me try it." He cupped his hands around his mouth and shouted, "Hey, loser!" Back came the echo, "Hey, loser!" Joe shouted again, "You're a waste of time!" Back came the echo, "You're a waste of time!"

"Wait a minute," Joe's father said. "Try saying something you'd like to hear."

"Okay," replied Joe. This time he shouted, "You're cool!" The echo answered, "You're cool!" "Let's be friends!" Joe shouted. Again the echo responded, "Let's be friends!"

"You know, Joe," his dad said, "people are a lot like that echo."

"What? How are people like an echo?" asked Joe.

"Well," his father replied, "when you talk mean to them, they usually talk mean back to you. But if you say nice things to them, they usually say nice things back."

Joe thought for a moment and said, "I'll remember that." As they rode away he shouted over his shoulder, "It was great talking to you!" The echo answered, "It was great talking to you!"

Remember to follow the Golden Rule: Treat people like you want to be treated. It's the best way to make friends.

The Royal Rangers Emblem

The Gold Points

The four gold points on the Royal Rangers Emblem remind us of how we grow: (1) physically, (2) spiritually, (3) mentally, and (4) socially.

Physical growth means that we grow in our body. We should get plenty of sleep, eat food that's good for us, and get a lot of exercise so that we will grow a strong healthy body.

Spiritual growth means we become more and more the kind of person Jesus wants us to be. We love Him, our parents, and others more. We read and study the Bible more and we love our church more. We do more things that please Jesus and fewer things that displease Him.

Mental growth means that our minds grow. We look, we listen, we read, we study. We put more and more knowledge into our minds. As our minds grow, we learn faster, understand better, and learn more about how to use what we know.

Social growth means we learn how to get along with other people. We learn to live by the Golden Rule and to try to be polite and helpful at all times.

The Red Points

The four red points of the Royal Rangers Emblem remind us of four important things the Church teaches: 1) Salvation, 2) Baptism in the Holy Spirit, 3) Healing, and 4) Rapture.

Salvation is a word that means we have accepted the Lord Jesus Christ as our personal Savior. We ask Jesus to forgive our sins. He forgives us and promises us eternal life with Him. We promise to love and serve Him. He lives in us and with us.

The Baptism in the Holy Spirit is a gift God offers to all believers. After we have invited Christ into our hearts, God wants to fill us with His Holy Spirit. (You'll find more about this in the last chapter of this handbook.)

Healing means we believe it is possible for Jesus to make us well when we are sick.

The Rapture will happen one day. When Jesus was on earth, He promised that He would come back for those who believed in Him. Someday Jesus will appear in the clouds. He will take all of His people back to heaven with Him.

The Blue Points

The eight blue points of the Royal Rangers Emblem represent the eight rules of the Royal Ranger Code. A code is a set of rules to follow, or live by. The Royal Ranger Code is a set of rules that Rangers do their best to live by each day.

A Royal Ranger is Alert

He is mentally, physically, and spiritually alert.

God has given each of us a mind and the ability to think. An alert Ranger is one who uses his ability to think to better himself mentally, physically, and spiritually.

A Royal Ranger is Clean

He is clean in body, mind, and speech.

A Ranger keeps his body clean. He takes a bath or a shower, shampoos his hair, brushes his teeth, and washes his hands and face. If possible, he should take a bath or shower each day, wash his hands before each meal and brush his teeth afterwards, and clean his fingernails each day. A clean body helps keep you healthy. It helps your Christian testimony and shows that you are trying to be a good Royal Ranger.

A clean mind means no bad thoughts allowed. We do not let them live in our minds. To keep this from happening, don't read, listen to, or look at anything that would put unclean thoughts into your mind.

A Ranger keeps his talk clean. He doesn't use bad

words. What a person says usually shows what is on the inside. If he speaks unclean words, it means he is unclean on the inside.

A Royal Ranger is Honest

He does not lie, cheat, or steal.

Sometimes a person lies and then covers it up by telling more lies. If he does this for very long, he starts to have trouble telling the difference between what is true and what is not. It is best to always tell the truth. Then we will never have to worry about telling a lie to cover up another lie.

Cheating is always wrong. A Ranger should not cheat in games, in sports, or in classwork. A person who cheats has a weak character. A person who does not cheat has a very strong character.

One of God's commands is "Do not steal." Remember the Golden Rule. Would you want someone to steal from you?

A Royal Ranger is Courageous

He is brave in spite of danger, criticism, or threats.

Being a daredevil does not prove someone is courageous. Sometimes being a daredevil shows how foolish someone is. To have

23

courage does not always mean to have no fear. Real courage is saying or doing what should be done even if we are afraid.

Sometimes it takes more courage to not do something. When we say "no" to the sinful things that others are doing, this takes courage. When we believe God's truth and others do not, this takes courage too.

A Royal Ranger is Loyal

He is faithful to his church, family, outpost, and friends.

A Ranger is loyal to his church when he goes to its Sunday school and worship services. He is loyal when he gives in the offerings. He is loyal when he says good things about his Sunday school, his church, and his pastor.

A Ranger is loyal to his home by obeying his parents. He is loyal when he shows kindness and thoughtfulness to his family. He is loyal when he prays for them. He is loyal when he speaks well of his home and family. He adds to his family's home life when he is cheerful and good-natured.

A Ranger is loyal to his outpost when he goes to its meetings. He is loyal when he cooperates with his leaders. He is loyal when he helps the other boys in his group. He is loyal when he works hard on his advancements and does all he can to make his group the best.

A Ranger is loyal to his friends. He helps them and prays for them each day.

A Royal Ranger is Courteous

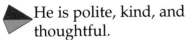

He is polite, kind, and thoughtful.

Being courteous is doing something that shows respect or consideration. We are showing respect when we say "yes, sir" and "no, sir" or "yes, ma'am" and "no, ma'am." We are showing consideration when we hold a door open for an older person. We are being polite when we say "please" and "thank you." Make a habit of doing what is polite, thoughtful, and respectful; then you will become a courteous person.

Being a gentleman is no sign of weakness. Some of the greatest men of all times knew how to be courteous. To be a top-notch Royal Ranger, always be a gentleman. We show respect when we address our leader as "Commander (your commander's name)."

A Royal Ranger is Obedient

He obeys his parents, leaders, and those in authority.

This story may help you understand obedience better.

One sunny day a boy was playing in the vacant lot near his house. He was sitting on the

ground when he heard his father say quietly, "Be perfectly still, and don't move." The boy was afraid, but he showed courage by doing as his father told him. The next moment he heard a shot. A rattlesnake had been coiled nearby, ready to strike. If the boy had moved, the snake would have bitten him. His courage in obeying saved his life. He was glad he had learned to obey.

There were two reasons for the boy's obedience. One, he was in the habit of obeying his father. Two, his father loved him and he loved his father. Willing obedience is one of the best ways to show love and respect to parents, to leaders, and to God.

A Royal Ranger is Spiritual

He prays, reads the Bible, and witnesses.

This is the most important point in the Royal Ranger Code. A Ranger does his best to be the kind of Christian Jesus wants him to be.

If you have a good friend, you enjoy talking to him. Jesus is the best friend anyone ever had. So talk to Him in prayer every day. Prayer is just talking to God.

When you pray, thank the Lord Jesus for His blessings, the good things in your life. Pray and ask Him to help you to be the kind of boy He wants you to be. Then ask Him to take care of you. Also, don't forget to pray for others. You will feel good when you pray each day.

The Bible is the most important book in the world. It is God's Word. It

Spiritual

RANGER KIDS

can change lives. As we read the Bible, it builds our faith and makes us stronger Christians. Read the Bible every day.

Witnessing is telling others about the Lord Jesus Christ. Because He has become our best friend—saving us—we tell others about Him. Many people don't have good friends. They need to meet the world's best friend, Jesus. He showed how much He loved everyone when He died on the cross. We can show Jesus how much we love Him by telling others He can be their Savior.

RANGER KIDS

Alert
Clean
Honest
Courageous
Loyal
Courteous
Obedient
Spiritual

Chapter 2
Ranger Kids Advancement Trails

The Royal Rangers program promotes by grade. Ranger Kids is for boys in kindergarten, first grade, and second grade. Discovery Rangers is for boys in third, fourth, and fifth grades. Adventure Rangers is for boys in sixth, seventh, and eighth grades. Expedition Rangers is for boys in ninth, tenth, eleventh, and twelfth grades. Each grade has its own Advancement Trail to follow.

After you complete each advancement step on the Trail, tell your commander. He will date and initial your handbook to show your progress on the Trail. Some of the steps will also need the signature of your mom or dad.

The Ranger Kids Advancement Trail is based on the needs, interests, and characteristics of boys in kindergarten, first grade, and second grade. The Trail is a plan of advancement through learning—from both experiences and activities—and being recognized for this learning. It is designed to offer every boy adventure and fun. The Trail is more than an interesting course of action; it is a new experience— a new achievement. It is a Ranger's opportunity to grow through new abilities, knowledge, and desires.

The *Ranger Kids Workbook* is to be

used with the *Ranger Kids Handbook*. The *Workbook* will help you learn about Rangers and remember what you have learned. You will enjoy coloring pictures, playing games, and completing each page. Your commander will keep your *Workbook* and will keep track of the advancements you complete.

We are going to learn lots of things together. I want to show you all that you can earn over the next three years. It's going to be exciting, so get ready.

Besides following the Advancement Trails, you can earn achievement awards. Each series of patches is a different color and has a different meaning. (Later on you will find out what you need to do to earn these awards.)

Patches with blue edges show you what a Royal Ranger should be. You will learn to be the best Christian you can be.

Patches with black edges teach about things around us. You will learn about history, people, and how to help others.

Patches with silver edges teach about things we do. Royal Rangers do a lot and are always learning more.

Patches with gold edges will teach important things about church. You can go to church and help out, and earn awards at the same time.

Patches with green edges tell about the outdoors and games. You will learn to take care of God's world.

Patches with red edges show how to help others. You will learn to be one of God's helpers.

Kindergarten
Trail to the Elk

   When you have earned the Antelope Award, the
Ram Award, the Caribou Award, and the Buffalo
Award, you have completed the requirements for the
Elk Award and will receive a patch. It can go on your
red uniform shirt, centered on the left pocket.

My Check-Off List for the Antelope Award

Physical

Clean around the
church for one month.

_____ _____
Commander's Signature   Date

Make a patrol flag.

_____ _____
Commander's Signature   Date

Spiritual

Memorize John 15:12.

_____ _____
Commander's Signature   Date

Memorize Romans 12:10.

_____ _____
Commander's Signature   Date

Mental

Learn the pledge to
the Christian flag.

_____ _____
Commander's Signature   Date

Learn the blue point Alert.

_____ _____
Commander's Signature   Date

Social

Learn the name and
address of your church.

_____ _____
Commander's Signature   Date

Go to one outpost activity.

_____ _____
Commander's Signature   Date

My Check-Off List for the Ram Award

Physical

Help the commander set up and clean the room for one month.

Commander's Signature	Date

Make a patrol collage.

Commander's Signature	Date

Spiritual

Memorize Proverbs 18:10.

Commander's Signature	Date

Memorize Romans 1:16.

Commander's Signature	Date

Mental

Learn the pledge to the United States flag.

Commander's Signature	Date

Learn the blue point Loyal.

Commander's Signature	Date

Social

Learn your pastor's name.

Commander's Signature	Date

Go to one outpost activity.

Commander's Signature	Date

My Check-Off List for the Caribou Award

Physical

Do a chore at home for one month.

_____ _____
Commander's Signature   Date

Make a poster on fire safety.

_____ _____
Commander's Signature   Date

Spiritual

Memorize Ephesians 6:1.

_____ _____
Commander's Signature   Date

Memorize Leviticus 19:32.

_____ _____
Commander's Signature   Date

Mental

Learn the song "Wherever I Go, God Is With Me."

_____ _____
Commander's Signature   Date

Learn the blue point Honest.

_____ _____
Commander's Signature   Date

Social

Name two dads in the Bible.

_____ _____
Commander's Signature   Date

Go to one outpost activity.

_____ _____
Commander's Signature   Date

My Check-Off List for the Buffalo Award

Physical

Clean around the church for one month.

_____
Commander's Signature   Date

Make a walking stick.

_____
Commander's Signature   Date

Spiritual

Memorize Genesis 1:1.

_____
Commander's Signature   Date

Memorize Psalm 139:14.

_____
Commander's Signature   Date

Mental

Learn the song "In the Beginning."

_____
Commander's Signature   Date

Learn the blue point Spiritual.

_____
Commander's Signature   Date

Social

Name three creations from the Bible.

_____
Commander's Signature   Date

Go to one outpost activity.

_____
Commander's Signature   Date

First Grade
Trail to the Wolverine

When you have earned the Beaver Award, the Fox Award, the Coyote Award, and the Badger Award, you have completed the requirements for the Wolverine Award and will receive a patch. It can go on your red uniform shirt, centered on the left pocket. It replaces the Elk Award you earned in kindergarten.

My Check-Off List for the Beaver Award

Physical

Clean around the church for one month.

```
_____  _____
Commander's Signature      Date
```

Make a patrol flag.

```
_____  _____
Commander's Signature      Date
```

Spiritual

Memorize Matthew 28:19.

```
_____  _____
Commander's Signature      Date
```

Memorize 1 Corinthians 16:13,14.

```
_____  _____
Commander's Signature      Date
```

Memorize Matthew 5:16.

```
_____  _____
Commander's Signature      Date
```

Mental

Learn the song "Jesus Loves the Little Children."

```
_____  _____
Commander's Signature      Date
```

Learn the blue point Courteous.

```
_____  _____
Commander's Signature      Date
```

Social

Name two missionaries.

```
_____  _____
Commander's Signature      Date
```

Go to one outpost activity.

```
_____  _____
Commander's Signature      Date
```

My Check-Off List for the Fox Award

Physical

Help the commander set up and clean the room for one month.

Commander's Signature	Date

Make a patrol collage.

Commander's Signature	Date

Spiritual

Memorize Psalm 23.

Commander's Signature	Date

Mental

Learn the song "Psalm 23."

Commander's Signature	Date

Learn the blue point Courageous.

Commander's Signature	Date

Social

List five rules to obey at home.

Commander's Signature	Date

Go to one outpost activity.

Commander's Signature	Date

My Check-Off List for the Coyote Award

Physical

Do a chore at home for one month.

Commander's Signature   Date

Make a poster on traffic safety.

Commander's Signature   Date

Spiritual

Memorize John 14:15.

Commander's Signature   Date

Memorize 1 Timothy 4:12.

Commander's Signature   Date

Memorize Psalm 119:11.

Commander's Signature   Date

Mental

Learn the song "Jesus, You Are Lord."

Commander's Signature   Date

Learn the blue point Obedient.

Commander's Signature   Date

Social

Name two famous hunters in the Bible.

Commander's Signature   Date

Go to one outpost activity.

Commander's Signature   Date

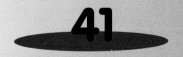

My Check-Off List for the Badger Award

Physical

Collect recyclables around the church for one month.

```
_____ _____
Commander's Signature   Date
```

Make a walking stick.

```
_____ _____
Commander's Signature   Date
```

Spiritual

Memorize Colossians 3:23.

```
_____ _____
Commander's Signature   Date
```

Memorize Genesis 1:28.

```
_____ _____
Commander's Signature   Date
```

Memorize Psalm 34:12,13.

```
_____ _____
Commander's Signature   Date
```

Mental

Learn the song "He's Got the Whole World in His Hands."

```
_____ _____
Commander's Signature   Date
```

Learn the blue point Clean.

```
_____ _____
Commander's Signature   Date
```

Social

Name the four Gospels during a group meeting.

```
_____ _____
Commander's Signature   Date
```

Go to one outpost activity.

```
_____ _____
Commander's Signature   Date
```

Second Grade
Trail to the Cougar

When you have earned the Lynx Award, the Cheetah Award, the Panther Award, and the Tiger Award, you have completed the requirements for the Cougar Award and will receive a patch. It can go on your red uniform shirt, centered on the left pocket. It replaces the Wolverine Award you earned in first grade.

43

My Check-Off List for the Lynx Award

Physical

Do a chore at home for one month.

_____ _____
Commander's Signature   Date

Make a patrol flag.

_____ _____
Commander's Signature   Date

Spiritual

Memorize the Golden Rule (Matthew 7:12).

_____ _____
Commander's Signature   Date

Memorize Matthew 7:13,14.

_____ _____
Commander's Signature   Date

Memorize Acts 1:8.

_____ _____
Commander's Signature   Date

Mental

Learn the song "Amazing Grace."

_____ _____
Commander's Signature   Date

Learn the gold point Spiritual.

_____ _____
Commander's Signature   Date

Learn the red point Salvation.

_____ _____
Commander's Signature   Date

Social

Bring two friends to Royal Rangers.

_____ _____
Commander's Signature   Date

Go to one outpost activity.

_____ _____
Commander's Signature   Date

My Check-Off List for the Cheetah Award

Physical

Help the commander set up and clean the room for one month.

Commander's Signature   Date

Make a patrol collage.

Commander's Signature   Date

Spiritual

Memorize John 3:16.

Commander's Signature   Date

Memorize Zephaniah 3:12.

Commander's Signature   Date

Memorize John 20:31.

Commander's Signature   Date

Mental

Learn the pledge to the Bible.

Commander's Signature   Date

Learn the gold point Physical.

Commander's Signature   Date

Learn the red point Healing.

Commander's Signature   Date

Social

Learn the names of all commanders in your outpost.

Commander's Signature   Date

Go to one outpost activity.

Commander's Signature   Date

45

My Check-Off List for the Panther Award

Physical

Do a chore at home for one month.

```
_____  _____
Commander's Signature    Date
```

Make a poster of your church—its people, ministries, and building.

```
_____  _____
Commander's Signature    Date
```

Spiritual

Memorize the Lord's Prayer (Matthew 6:9–13).

```
_____  _____
Commander's Signature    Date
```

Mental

Learn the song "Trust and Obey."

```
_____  _____
Commander's Signature    Date
```

Learn the gold point Mental.

```
_____  _____
Commander's Signature    Date
```

Learn the red point Baptism in the Holy Spirit.

```
_____  _____
Commander's Signature    Date
```

Social

Name three disciples during a group meeting.

```
_____  _____
Commander's Signature    Date
```

Go to one outpost activity.

```
_____  _____
Commander's Signature    Date
```

My Check-Off List for
the Tiger Award

Physical

Pick up trash around the
church for one month.

_____ _____
Commander's Signature   Date

Make a walking stick.

_____ _____
Commander's Signature   Date

Spiritual

Memorize Psalm 119:105.

_____ _____
Commander's Signature   Date

Memorize Matthew 6:26.

_____ _____
Commander's Signature   Date

Memorize James 1:17.

_____ _____
Commander's Signature   Date

Mental

Learn the song "Ready."

_____ _____
Commander's Signature   Date

Learn the gold point Social.

_____ _____
Commander's Signature   Date

Learn the red point Rapture.

_____ _____
Commander's Signature   Date

Social

Name the closest national forest.

_____ _____
Commander's Signature   Date

Go to one outpost activity.

_____ _____
Commander's Signature   Date

Chapter 3
Ranger Kids Achievement Awards

Have you been busy working on your advancements? Here are some achievement awards that you can earn. Your commander will help you earn some of them at the meetings. But there are many more that you can earn at home, at school, or on trips with your mom, dad, or group. So look ahead and see what fun is in store.

Your commander or parents can write their initials in the box when you have completed a step of the achievement award. Sometimes you may miss a week or two of Royal Rangers. You may have joined Royal Rangers after the group had worked on an award. You can still earn that award. Your mom, dad, grandparent—almost anyone—can help you earn it. After you complete all the steps and have all the boxes initialed, you have earned that award. Then you can wear the patch on your shirt. I hope you have fun. If you have any questions, ask your commander.

One type of award you can earn is the Commander's Choice awards. These can be given for events not covered in the achievement awards. The Commander's Choice awards may be earned for doing ministry, home, or community activities. The following is a guide for earning these awards.

 1. **Physical:** You do some physical labor or activity promoting an event or learning more about it.

 2. **Spiritual:** You learn a spiritual lesson. This may happen through prayer, reading or memorizing a Scripture passage, or going to church.

 3. **Mental:** You do a mental activity. You can tell about something you did, show how to do something, or discuss something.

 4. **Social:** You take part with others your age or with adults in developing social skills, such as speaking in front of a group or working on a project with others.

There are 48 achievement awards. You may work on these at home and in your Ranger Kids meetings.

ADVENTURES ON WHEELS

Earned during the Tiger quarter

- [ ] **Physical:** Go to a bike rally, skateboard meet, Pinewood Derby, or any other event having to do with wheels.

- [ ] **Spiritual:** For a week, pray about how God can use you and your bike, skateboard, Pinewood Derby car, or other wheels to tell others about Jesus.

- [ ] **Mental:** Draw a picture of what you did at the event. Display it at a meeting. Your picture should promote the event and Royal Rangers.

- [ ] **Social:** Clean up the event area. Work with other boys to do this.

ARTS

Earned during the Lynx quarter

- [ ] **Physical:** Make two of the following four: sculpture, drawing, painting, collage.

- [ ] **Spiritual:** Read or have someone read Psalm 139 to you.

- [ ] **Mental:** Choose the art piece you would like to display. Explain to your commander or parent why you chose that piece.

- [ ] **Social:** Display one of your pieces of art and explain how you made it.

BE A FRIEND

Earned during the Cheetah quarter

- [ ] **Physical:** Make friends with three people you do not know. Invite them to church or to Royal Rangers.

- [ ] **Spiritual:** Read or have someone read to you the story of Jonathan and David in 1 Samuel 20.

- [ ] **Mental:** Explain to your commander or parent how to be a friend.

- [ ] **Social:** Introduce your friend to Royal Rangers, and tell the group how you met.

BUDDY BARREL

Earned during the Lynx quarter

- **Physical:** Go to a Boys and Girls Missionary Crusade (BGMC) event or help a leader with a BGMC event.
- **Spiritual:** Memorize 1 John 3:7.
- **Mental:** Think of two ways to raise money for your Buddy Barrel. Tell the two ways to your commander or parent.
- **Social:** Hand out brochures advertising the BGMC event. Tell others about it.

CHURCH HELPER

Earned during the Antelope quarter

- **Physical:** For one month, do four different chores around the church. Talk to your commander or pastor about what you can do.
- **Spiritual:** Read or have someone read Luke 4:14–21 to you.
- **Mental:** Draw a picture of your church.
- **Social:** Explain the chores you performed at church and what the experience did for you and others. Display your picture in your group meeting.

CHURCH HISTORY

Earned during the Antelope quarter

- **Physical:** Visit your pastor or a church member who can tell you how your church started.
- **Spiritual:** Pray every day for one month for your pastor and your church.
- **Mental:** Make a collage of pictures of your church and those who have worked in it. Ask your parent or commander for help.
- **Social:** Tell the boys in your group how you prayed for the church and the pastor.

CLEAN BODY

Earned during the Caribou quarter

☐ **Physical:** For one month, do the four things you listed under Mental.

☐ **Spiritual:** Read or have someone read John 13:1–17 to you.

☐ **Mental:** With the help of your parent or commander, list four ways you can keep your body clean.

☐ **Social:** Explain to the group why it is important to keep our bodies clean.

COMMUNITY HELPER

Earned during the Beaver quarter

☐ **Physical:** Do a good deed in your community, such as picking up trash in a park.

☐ **Spiritual:** Read or have someone read to you Luke 19:1–10, the story of Zacchaeus.

☐ **Mental:** Plan your good deed with your commander or parent. If necessary, get permission from the appropriate community authority.

☐ **Social:** Tell your group what deed you did and the importance of being a community helper.

COOKING

Earned during the Badger quarter

☐ **Physical:** Prepare a meal for your family and a simple meal for your group.

☐ **Spiritual:** Read or have someone read to you the story of Elijah in 1 Kings 17:1–16.

☐ **Mental:** Write a menu and have it approved by your commander or parent. It must be a balanced meal based on the Food Guide Pyramid.

☐ **Social:** Tell your group how you prepared the meal.

CRAFT

Earned during the Ram quarter

☐ **Physical:** Make three crafts at home or at your Ranger Kids meetings.

☐ **Spiritual:** Have someone read to you the story of Bezalel and Oholiab in Exodus 35:30 to 36:5.

☐ **Mental:** Spend time talking about your craft projects with a commander or parent.

☐ **Social:** Show your crafts at a meeting. Tell the group about one project you made.

DAY CAMP

Earned during the Badger quarter

☐ **Physical:** Go to a day camp sponsored by Royal Rangers.

☐ **Spiritual:** Invite a friend to the day camp. Explain to him what you do in Royal Rangers and how it helps you to be a better Christian.

☐ **Mental:** Complete all the crafts and projects at the day camp.

☐ **Social:** Help the commanders set up or clean up at the day camp.

DEFENDER OF THE WORD

Earned during the Fox quarter

☐ **Physical**: Go to or watch a program about the Bible.

☐ **Spiritual**: Read or have someone read to you 1 Timothy 4.

☐ **Mental**: Paint a picture that explains that the Bible is God's Word.

☐ **Social**: Explain to your group why you believe the Bible. Display your painting in your group meeting.

DOER OF THE WORD

Earned during the Fox quarter

Physical: Choose one of the following to do: join a Junior Bible Quiz (JBQ) team, hand out Bibles at church or in a neighborhood, go to Vacation Bible School.

Spiritual: Read or have someone read to you the story of Josiah in 2 Kings 22.

Mental: Draw a picture that shows how important the Bible is to you.

Social: Talk to your group about the importance of the Bible.

FAMILY HISTORY

Earned during the Caribou quarter

Physical: Visit a relative to learn some family history. For example, ask your grandmother to tell stories about when she was your age.

Spiritual: Read or have someone read to you Genesis 45.

Mental: With the help of a parent or grandparent, make your family tree and include back to your grandparents.

Social: Tell your group a story that you heard from your relative.

FIREFIGHTER

Earned during the Caribou quarter

Physical: Visit a fire department or have a firefighter visit your outpost.

Spiritual: Read or have someone read to you 1 Kings 18:16–39, the story about Elijah and the prophets of Baal.

Mental: Draw a floor plan of your house. Show the routes your family would follow to escape during a fire. Put an "X" outside where everyone would meet.

Social: With your family, check all the smoke detectors in your house.

FLAG

Earned during the Fox quarter

☐ **Physical:** For one month, take part in flag ceremonies at Royal Rangers.

☐ **Spiritual:** Learn the pledge to the United States flag.

☐ **Mental:** On a large piece of paper, plan and draw a large picture of the United States flag.

☐ **Social:** Ask the commander to tell you a story of a war veteran who served his country. Tell that story to other boys or to your family.

GAMES

Earned during the Buffalo quarter

☐ **Physical:** Teach your friends from school or the neighborhood a game you learned at Royal Rangers.

☐ **Spiritual:** Memorize Proverbs 18:24.

☐ **Mental:** Learn to play three board games.

☐ **Social:** Teach your group how to play one game.

GOD IS WORKING

Earned during the Cheetah quarter

☐ **Physical:** Take a tour around the church to see where all its ministries take place.

☐ **Spiritual:** Memorize Matthew 28:19,20.

☐ **Mental:** Make a painting that shows how much God loves the world.

☐ **Social:** Show your painting to your group and explain what it means.

GOING PLACES

Earned during the Coyote quarter

☐ **Physical:** Take three trips, each using a different method of travel. For example, go by bus, by bicycle, and by walking.

☐ **Spiritual:** Read or have someone read to you the story of Saul's travels in 1 Samuel 9:1 to 10:8

☐ **Mental:** Explain to a commander or parent how each way of traveling was different.

☐ **Social:** Tell the boys in your group about one of your trips.

GOVERNMENT

Earned during the Beaver quarter

☐ **Physical:** Visit a city, county, state, or federal building. Or color and identify the White House and Capitol Building.

☐ **Spiritual:** Read or have someone read Romans 13 to you.

☐ **Mental:** Tell a commander the name of the United States president, the name of your state's governor, and the name of a government office holder in your town or county.

☐ **Social:** Tell the group what you saw at the building you visited. Or tell them something you know about the president of the United States.

HELP A NEIGHBOR

Earned during the Beaver quarter

☐ **Physical:** Talk with your parent and a neighbor about doing a chore around the neighbor's house.

☐ **Spiritual:** Every day for one week, pray for the neighbor you are helping.

☐ **Mental:** Each day after doing the chore, talk to your neighbor for a few minutes.

☐ **Social:** Tell your group what you did and how the neighbor responded.

HELP THE COMMANDER

Earned during the Ram quarter

- [ ] **Physical:** Learn what an assistant patrol guide or a patrol guide does.

- [ ] **Spiritual:** Read or have someone read Exodus 18 to you.

- [ ] **Mental:** List five great leaders of history, including leaders in the Bible.

- [ ] **Social:** Tell your parent, commander, or your group a story about a leader you like.

HISTORY

Earned during the Lynx quarter

- [ ] **Physical:** Take a trip with your group or parent to a historical marker or site.

- [ ] **Spiritual:** Read or have someone read to you the story of Joshua and the Israelites in Joshua 4.

- [ ] **Mental:** Make a picture or sculpture of a historical marker or gravestone.

- [ ] **Social:** Explain to your group what was important about the site you visited.

HOME HELPER

Earned during the Caribou quarter

- [ ] **Physical:** For four days do the chores that you listed in the Mental section.

- [ ] **Spiritual:** Read or have someone read to you John 13:1–17.

- [ ] **Mental:** Write down three chores that you will do around the house.

- [ ] **Social:** Tell the group about the chores you did and how you felt when you finished them.

57

IN THE AIR

Earned during the Cheetah quarter

☐ **Physical:** With your group or parent, take a trip to the airport or an air show.

☐ **Spiritual:** Read or have someone read to you Revelation 21.

☐ **Mental:** Draw or make a kite.

☐ **Social:** Tell your group what you liked most about the airport or air show.

JOYFUL NOISE

Earned during the Antelope quarter

☐ **Physical:** Go to or view a musical concert. It can be singing, playing musical instruments, or both. Select either Christian or classical music.

☐ **Spiritual:** Read or have someone read to you Psalm 100.

☐ **Mental:** For two weeks practice a song you will sing or play for your group.

☐ **Social:** Sing or play a song for your group.

KEEPER OF THE LAW

Earned during the Coyote quarter

☐ **Physical:** Visit a police station or interview a police officer.

☐ **Spiritual:** Read or have someone read to you Acts 23:12–22.

☐ **Mental:** Draw a picture of you obeying the law.

☐ **Social:** Tell the group one important thing you learned at the police station or from the police officer.

LIGHT FOR THE LOST

Earned during the Lynx quarter

☐ **Physical:** Go to a Light for the Lost (LFTL) event or learn about LFTL at a Ranger meeting.

☐ **Spiritual:** Read or have someone read to you a story about a missionary being helped by LFTL.

☐ **Mental:** Work with a leader to think of a way to raise money for LFTL.

☐ **Social:** Help a commander or a LFTL team member during the LFTL event.

MAP

Earned during the Cheetah quarter

☐ **Physical:** Take a trip with your parent from your home to the closest police station, to the church, and back to your home.

☐ **Spiritual:** Read or have someone read to you Joshua 18:1–10.

☐ **Mental:** With the help of a commander or parent, draw a map of your trip. Use proper map codes and directions.

☐ **Social:** Explain to your group how to read a map.

MONEY HELPER

Earned during the Coyote quarter

☐ **Physical:** Go to the store with your group or parent to buy items needed for an outpost activity or for a meal in your home.

☐ **Spiritual:** Read or have someone read to you Ezra 1:1–11, a story of God taking care of His people.

☐ **Mental:** Work with your commander or parent to put together a list of items and their cost for the outpost activity or home meal. (No cooking should be needed for the outpost activity.)

☐ **Social:** Serve the items to the boys in your group or guests in your home.

NATURE

Earned during the Tiger quarter

☐ **Physical:** Go on a hike. Collect leaves, rocks, or other items of nature without harming anything.

☐ **Spiritual:** Read or have someone read to you Psalm 148.

☐ **Mental:** Make a display of your collection. Write down the names of the items.

☐ **Social:** Show your collection at a meeting. Tell about what you collected.

NOAH'S ARK

Earned during the Buffalo quarter

☐ **Physical:** Go to a park or a nearby wooded area with your group or parent. Look for and listen to animals, including birds.

☐ **Spiritual:** Read or have someone read to you Jonah 1:17 to 2:10.

☐ **Mental:** Draw pictures or make a list of all the animals you saw or heard during your outing.

☐ **Social:** Tell the boys in your group what you saw and heard, and show your pictures.

OLD WEST

Earned during the Badger quarter

☐ **Physical:** Attend a Western Day event where you learn about the ways of the Old West and participate in games and activities.

☐ **Spiritual:** Read or have someone read to you 1 Samuel 24.

☐ **Mental:** Draw a picture of all the things that you did at the event.

☐ **Social:** Invite two friends to go to the event.

OUTING

Earned during the Buffalo quarter

Physical: Plan and go on an outing outside of your area. Some examples of outings are a campout, a trip to the zoo, or a visit to your grandparent's home.

Spiritual: Read or have someone read to you Acts 11:19–26.

Mental: Draw pictures or make a journal about your trip.

Social: Tell your group about your trip.

PATROL HELPER

Earned during the Coyote quarter

Physical: Take part in four opening or closing ceremony drills.

Spiritual: Read or have someone read to you Joshua 6:1–20.

Mental: Take part in the planning of the four drills.

Social: Tell the boys in your group why teamwork is important.

PUPPET

Earned during the Panther quarter

Physical: Make a puppet for a skit. John 6 might have a story for your skit or puppet show.

Spiritual: Read or have someone read to you John 6:1–15.

Mental: Prepare a show or skit having at least two speaking characters.

Social: Perform a puppet show or a skit for your group.

RANGERS ABOUT TOWN

Earned during the Buffalo quarter

[ ] **Physical:** Wear your uniform to a community festival or parade.

[ ] **Spiritual:** Read or have someone read to you 1 Kings 8:62–66 and Luke 19:28–40.

[ ] **Mental:** Draw a picture of the parade or festival that you attended.

[ ] **Social:** With help from a commander or parent, buy candy and hand it to people in the crowd at the festival or parade.

SAFETY

Earned during the Beaver quarter

[ ] **Physical:** Practice a fire drill in a meeting. Practice a fire drill at home.

[ ] **Spiritual:** Read or have someone read to you Psalm 91.

[ ] **Mental:** Learn what to do in case of
   1) fire,   4) medical emergency, or
   2) tornado,   5) physical abuse.
   3) earthquake,

[ ] **Social:** Explain to your group how to keep their homes or the church safe.

SCHOOL

Earned during the Panther quarter

[ ] **Physical:** For one month, follow the plan you made to improve in a school subject.

[ ] **Spiritual:** Memorize 2 Timothy 2:15.

[ ] **Mental:** Choose a school subject in which you need to improve. With your parent, plan a regular time to meet for help.

[ ] **Social:** Tell how studying helped you make better grades.

SPORTING EVENT

Earned during the Fox quarter

Physical: Go to a sporting event in your community with a parent or your group.

Spiritual: Ask God to bless your time with your parent or group. Pray this each day for a week.

Mental: Make a poster from the event. Use items like your ticket, a candy bar wrapper, a program.

Social: Tell your group about attending the sporting event.

SPORTS

Earned during the Tiger quarter

Physical: For four weeks, take part in a sports event held at the church.

Spiritual: Read or have someone read to you Isaiah 40:27–31.

Mental: Draw a picture of the sports event in which you took part.

Social: During the four weeks, show good sportsmanship and encourage your group members to show good sportsmanship.

STRONG BODY

Earned during the Ram quarter

Physical: For one month, do three exercises four days a week.

Spiritual: Memorize Hebrews 12:1.

Mental: Explain to your commander or parent how the exercises will help you to become stronger and healthier.

Social: Explain to your group the importance of physical fitness.

SUNDAY SCHOOL

Earned during the Antelope quarter

Physical: Go to Sunday school for at least 10 Sundays.

Spiritual: Learn the memory verse for each Sunday school lesson.

Mental: Draw a picture of your Sunday school teacher and give it to him or her.

Social: Invite two friends to Sunday school.

TAKING CARE OF GOD'S WORLD

Earned during the Badger quarter

Physical: Take a day hike to demonstrate the things listed in the Mental section.

Spiritual: Read or have someone read to you Genesis 1:1–31.

Mental: List or draw five ways you can save energy or protect our natural resources.

Social: Tell your group ways to save energy and our natural resources.

TELLING OTHERS ABOUT JESUS

Earned during the Panther quarter

Physical: With your group or your parent, plan an outing for witnessing, telling people about Jesus. Hand out tracts about Jesus and talk to people about Him.

Spiritual: Memorize Acts 1:8.

Mental: Explain the gospel—the good news of the Bible—to your commander.

Social: Tell your group what you did on your outing.

TYING KNOTS

Earned during the Tiger quarter

- **Physical:** Learn and make the following 3 knots: 1) figure eight, 2) square, and 3) overhand.
- **Spiritual:** Memorize Psalm 37:3.
- **Mental:** Demonstrate one knot to your commander and explain how you can use it.
- **Social:** Demonstrate for the group how to tie one knot.

WHAT'S ON TV

Earned during the Ram quarter

- **Physical:** After you memorize the Scripture verse in the Spiritual section, choose any two of the following, with parental permission: attend a play, watch a TV show or video.
- **Spiritual:** Memorize Philippians 4:8.
- **Mental:** Discuss with your parent or commander how you decide what is good to watch.
- **Social:** Explain to your group how to avoid watching movies and TV shows that are not good for you.

WORKING TOGETHER

Earned during the Panther quarter

- **Physical:** Help the commander with a game and demonstrate good team spirit for one month.
- **Spiritual:** Read or have someone read to you the story of Moses, Hur, and Joshua in Exodus 17:8–16.
- **Mental:** List four ways to improve team spirit in your group.
- **Social:** Discuss with your group ways to improve team spirit.

God and Me Award

Since you are in Ranger Kids, the God and Country program offers you another award you can earn besides those in the Royal Rangers program. It's called the God and Me Award. You learn the story of your life and you learn the story of Jesus' life. You learn how God puts the two stories together. When you complete the *God and Me Student Workbook,* you will receive a medal. You can wear it on the left pocket of your red uniform shirt above your advancement patch.

The God and Country program is used by many organizations, such as Boys Scouts, Girl Scouts, and Camp Fire Boys and Girls. It was put together by the National Commission for Church and Youth Agency Relationships. It offers other awards as you get older. The materials for the God and Country program can be ordered from Gospel Publishing House.

Would you like to earn this award? Then have your parent or your commander go through the course with you.

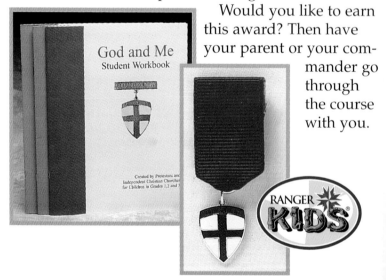

Chapter 4
Ranger Kids Uniforms

Royal Rangers wear uniforms to their meetings. Each group has its own uniform. Your Ranger Kids uniform shows you belong to Ranger Kids. Take good care of your uniform. You may want to hang it up when you get home so it will be ready for the next meeting. When your uniform is dirty, ask for help at home to get it clean. Look at these pictures to see what Ranger Kids uniforms look like.

Here are examples of Class C uniforms. This uniform is a Ranger Kids or Royal Rangers T-shirt, cap, and jeans or shorts. You can also wear your vest with this uniform to show all of your awards.

Class C Uniforms

This boy is wearing shorts with his Class C uniform. To avoid bug bites, wear long socks that cover and protect your legs. Always wear sturdy shoes or boots.

Class B Uniforms

The Class B uniform is a Ranger Kids shirt (long-sleeved, red shirt), a Ranger Kids bolo tie, and blue jeans. You may also wear your vest and Ranger Kids cap. Boys in Ranger Kids do not have a Class A uniform.

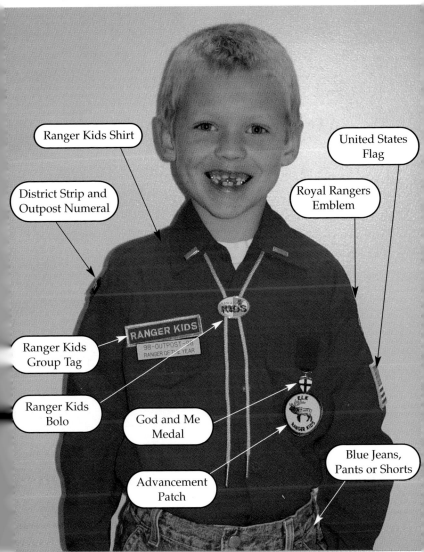

Ranger Kids Shirt

United States Flag

District Strip and Outpost Numeral

Royal Rangers Emblem

Ranger Kids Group Tag

Ranger Kids Bolo

God and Me Medal

Advancement Patch

Blue Jeans, Pants or Shorts

This boy is wearing the Class B uniform with the vest showing all of his awards.

Right Shoulder

District Strip—centered and 1/2″ below right shoulder seam

Outpost Numeral—centered flush with bottom of district strip

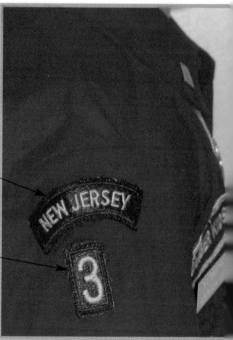

Left Shoulder

Royal Rangers Emblem (small emblem for Ranger Kids)— centered and $1/2''$ below left shoulder seam

United States Flag—centered and $1/2''$ below emblem. Royal Rangers in other countries should wear a patch of their nation's flag.

Collar

Assistant Patrol Guide Bar—centered on the collar $1/2''$ from the front edge of collar and parallel to the front edge of collar

Bolo Tie—centered and covering top button of shirt

Right Pocket

Ranger Kids Group Tag—centered and touching pocket

Ranger of the Year Name Tag—centered and flush with the top of the pocket

Activity or Commemorative Patch—centered top to bottom and side to side. You must have attended the event in order to wear the patch.

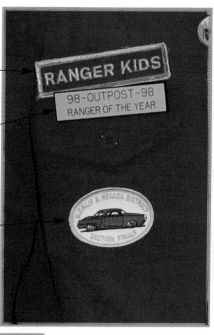

Left Pocket

God and Me Medal—centered and flush with the top of the pocket

Advancement Patch—centered top to bottom and side to side. Wear the highest advancement patch you have earned.

The Awards Vest

Boy's Right Front of Vest

Royal Rangers Emblem (small emblem for Ranger Kids)—centered and 3″ from top seam

Assistant Patrol Guide Bar

Advancement Patches—bottom of patches to be 2″ from bottom of vest. First patch touches the hem of vest and succeeding patches touch top to bottom and side to side. Use order seen here.

Boy's Left Front of Vest

Ranger Kids Emblem—centered and 3″ from top seam

Ranger of the Year Name Tag—centered

Advancement Patches

Medals—lined up along straight vertical line; maximum of 3 rows and 3 columns 6″ from bottom of vest

Activity Patches—same format as Advancement Patches

Back of the Vest

Achievement Patches—placed 2″ from top seam of vest and touching the preceding patch

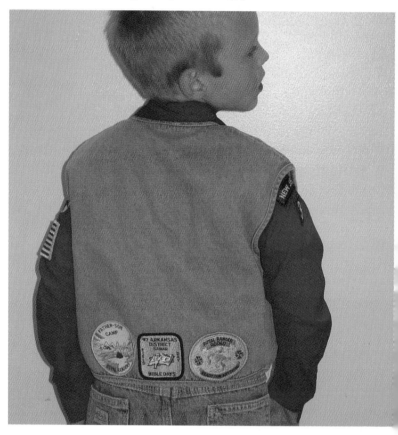

Activity Patches—placed along the bottom of the vest and touching the preceding patch

Chapter 5

Your Royal Rangers Outpost

RANGER KIDS

The Church Outpost

A great bunch of boys and leaders make up your church outpost. Your group is one of several in the outpost: Ranger Kids, Discovery Rangers, Adventure Rangers, and Expedition Rangers. These different groups may not meet at the same time or place. But they must have the same sponsoring church (or organization).

Patrols

Each group in the outpost is divided into patrols of five to eight boys. For example, if your Ranger Kids group has sixteen members, it can have two patrols, each with eight members. Or it can have three patrols, two with five members and one with six members. Your patrol does activities together. You will work, learn, and play together. In this way, you will come to feel that you belong, that you are part of a team.

Ranger Kids Leadership

Being in Royal Rangers gives you many opportunities to grow. For example, your group will give you opportunities both to follow and to lead. Good followers generally make good leaders. Every group has its own leaders. Your group has leaders called guides. They are chosen by your commander or elected by your group.

A rope is strong only if all of its cords stay wrapped together. Work with the others in your group and follow the leaders. Then your group will be strong like a new rope. To become a leader, learn how to help the group. Think about what they should be doing next. You can learn to lead. Let Jesus lead you, and listen to the directions of those in charge.

The activities of your Ranger Kids group will open new doors to fun, adventure, and friendship.

Outpost Chaplain

The outpost chaplain may give devotions. He cares for other spiritual needs of the outpost. He may be the pastor of your church. The chaplain wears gold bars on his uniform.

Senior Commander

The senior commander is over all groups in the outpost. He plans and organizes their activities. He helps the other commanders in the outpost. He is given this job by the leaders of the church. He is responsible to the church for the outpost's overall development and progress. The senior commander wears white bars on his uniform.

Ranger Kids Commander

The Ranger Kids commander works with the other commanders. Together they plan all activities of the Ranger Kids, their meetings, day camps, projects, and assemblies. The commander is a person to respect. The commander will help you learn. The Ranger Kids commander can be a man or a woman, at least 21 years old. He or she works with the other group leaders who make up the entire Royal Rangers outpost. The commander wears a set of double blue bars on his or her uniform.

Lieutenant Commander

The lieutenant commander must be at least 18 years old. The lieutenant

commander helps the commander lead the group. During meetings he may be in charge of certain activities or parts of the meeting. When the commander is absent, the lieutenant commander takes charge. The Ranger Kids lieutenant commander can be a man or a woman. The commander wears a set of single blue bars on his or her uniform.

Patrol Guide

The patrol guide is appointed by the commander or elected by his patrol. He serves for three to six months at a time. He will serve no more than a full year at one time. The patrol guide leads by example. He is to lead his patrol in all activities. He works with the commander to help the patrol select a name, a flag, and a yell or song. The guide's duties include the following:

1. being a good Christian,
2. keeping patrol members informed,
3. getting the patrol to be a part of all group activities,
4. developing patrol spirit,
5. wearing a correct uniform, and
6. living by the Royal Ranger Code.

The patrol guide also leads his patrol in games at recreation time and is in charge of his patrol on hikes or when they are moving from one area to another.

The guide has duties when he marches with his patrol. He carries the patrol flag at the head of the line (or column). He leads them in their patrol song or yell. During outdoor assemblies or group roll call, he stands at the front or to the right of the row and reports for his patrol. The patrol guide should try to do his very best at all times. The patrol guide wears a set of double green bars on his uniform.

Assistant Patrol Guide

The assistant patrol guide is appointed by the commander or elected by his patrol. He serves for three to six months at a time. His title describes what he is supposed to do: he is to assist, or help, the patrol guide carry out his duties. The assistant guide should also be a good example by doing the following:

1. being a good Christian,
2. developing patrol spirit,
3. working with the other members,
4. wearing a correct uniform, and
5. living by the Royal Ranger Code.

If the guide is gone during meetings or activities, the assistant guide takes over until he returns. The assistant guide marches at the rear of the line (or column) of his patrol. He stands on the left end of the patrol row when the patrol lines up side by side. The assistant patrol guide wears a set of single green bars on his uniform.

Ranger Kids Patrols

A Time for Patrol Corners

Patrol Corners is one part of most Ranger Kids weekly meetings. This time is for planning and talking about things that everyone in your groups likes to do. You may work on advancements, patrol flags and songs, or plans of upcoming events. You can talk about what you need to do and projects that need to be done.

Encouraging Patrol Spirit

As a patrol member you help with the patrol spirit. Each patrol member is to care about the patrol as much as he cares about himself. He should put the patrol ahead of what he wants to do.

Patrol spirit makes your team work together. Patrol spirit can give excitement to whatever needs to be done. Patrol spirit makes you want to do your best. You do your part to keep on trying no matter how hard it seems to be.

Everyone in the patrol is special so treat each boy as a special person. Your patrol stands out from the others because you care about what happens to the patrol. You can give the patrol your best by doing these things:

1. be at every meeting,
2. wear a correct uniform,
3. sing your patrol song,
4. shout out the patrol yell,

5. work hard on patrol projects, and

6. respect your patrol guide's leadership.

Your Patrol Name

Each patrol chooses a name that everyone in the patrol likes—a name that is exciting. The name should describe a quality or characteristic you will be glad to have. Your group in Royal Rangers is called Ranger Kids. The awards you work for have names of wildlife. Names that describe wildlife—such as Soaring Eagles or Brave Bears—are good ideas for patrol names.

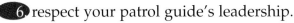

Your Patrol Flag

A patrol flag identifies your patrol, especially when you are with other patrols. You can use it to show patrol location, patrol equipment, and patrol projects. Patrol flags can be made by patrol members. Use your imagination. Work together. Design a flag that everyone in your patrol would want to carry in a parade. At the beginning of every year, your patrol makes a new flag with the help of your commander.

Your Patrol Song and Yell

Each patrol has a song and a yell. They are made up by the patrol. Your patrol will make up a song and a yell. They should be lively, with a beat. They should be easy to learn and sing. You can choose a tune you know already and add your own words. Patrol songs and yells will put life and excitement into every meeting.

Your Patrol Scrapbook

A patrol scrapbook is another fun project. It can include photographs, pictures, patches, ribbons—anything the patrol has done and finds interesting. Make the scrapbook a record of the fun and excitement you've had with your friends.

Outpost Assembly

Group and Patrol Formation

Ranger Kids need to know how to line up. You will be lining up at opening ceremonies, closing ceremonies, and assemblies. Everyone has a place to stand when the patrols come together in formation. The guides should know where and how their patrols are to line up.

Lining up is done in two ways:

1. One behind the other. The guide is at the front of the line. The assistant guide is at the back of the line.

2. Side by side. The guide is the last one on the right of the patrol and the assistant guide is the last one on the left.

The commander stands facing the group. His lieutenant commanders, if he has two, stand one to his left and one to his right. The patrol faces the commanders.

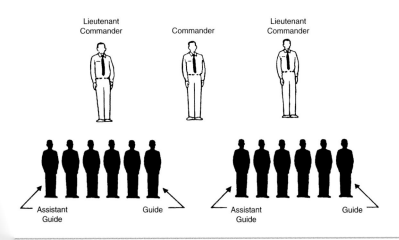

How To Fold the Flag

Folded Flag

Flag Raising

Flags are a part of Royal Rangers assemblies. The United States flag, the Christian flag, and the Royal Rangers flag may be raised by one of the patrols. Sometimes such a patrol is called a color guard ("colors" is another word for "flag"). First, the U.S. flag is quickly raised. Then the other flags are raised. When the U.S. flag is raised, do a hand salute if you are wearing your uniform. Your right hand goes to the top of your right eyebrow or to the brim of your cap. Do a heart salute if you are not wearing your uniform. Your right hand goes over your heart. After all the flags are raised, the commander leads the assembly in reciting the pledges to the U.S. and Christian flags and the Royal Ranger Pledge. The Christian flag is saluted with a heart salute. The Royal Ranger Pledge is recited with the right hand raised and the elbow bent.

Your commander may choose to recite the pledge to the Bible as part of the flag raising ceremony. Stand at attention as you recite the pledge to the Bible.

Pledges

Learning all of these pledges is part of your advancements. You will learn them as you earn your awards. Your commander will help you learn them in the meetings. Your mom or dad can also help you learn them at home.

UNITED STATES FLAG: "I pledge allegiance to the Flag of the United States of America, and to the Republic for which it stands; one Nation under God, indivisible, with liberty and justice for all."

CHRISTIAN FLAG: "I pledge allegiance to the Christian flag and to the Savior for whose Kingdom it stands; one brotherhood, uniting all true Christians in service and in love."

Royal Rangers do not give a pledge to the Royal Rangers flag. However, during flag raising ceremonies we say the Royal Ranger Pledge while facing the Royal Rangers flag.

ROYAL RANGER PLEDGE: "With God's help, I will do my best to serve God, my church, and my fellowman; to live by the Ranger Code; to make the Golden Rule my daily rule."

HOLY BIBLE: "I pledge allegiance to the Bible, God's Holy Word. I will make it a lamp unto my feet, and a light unto my path, and will hide its words in my heart that I might not sin against God."

RANGER KID

Chapter 6.
Safety and the Great Outdoors

Hiking wilderness trails holds great adventure! American Indians may have used the trails along a river long ago. Leaf-covered paths in the forest can take you into the world of bird calls, squirrel chatter, and more. Each turn in a mountain trail can reveal a new sight. Through nature studies, Royal Rangers will give you opportunities to learn about God's great creation—animals, birds, fish, trees, stars, and much more.

Wherever you are, you'll need to know about safety. Through Royal Rangers, you will learn

1. how to give first aid to someone who is injured or sick,

   what to do in an emergency, and

3. how to keep yourself safe.

Helping Others Through First Aid

First aid is the care you give to anyone who is hurt or sick. Your help can keep that injured or sick person from becoming worse until those with medical training arrive. First aid also includes treating minor injuries, such as small cuts and scrapes, so they don't get worse.

How To Help

Helping others requires knowing what to do and staying calm enough to do it. So learn what to do and then remember to ask God for peace during an emergency.

1. Check the victim and the area around the person. (The victim is the one who is hurt or sick.)

Looking at the person and the area might help you know what happened. Can you tell what the victim was doing when he became hurt or sick?

2. Call 911 or your local emergency number. Tell them at least these four things: 1) your name, 2) what happened, 3) where you are, and 4) what you know about the victim. It might sound like this: "My name is John Jones. A boy wrecked his bike at the bottom of a hill at 1200 South Main Street. The boy is awake, but his leg looks broken, and his knee is bleeding." Calling for help may be the most important thing you can do to help the person.

3. Care for the victim by giving first aid until medical help arrives. Never move someone who is seriously hurt unless he or she is in danger, such as fire, flood, or poisonous gas.

When someone has difficulty breathing, call 911 right away. If that person stops breathing, he or she will need help to breathe. You may be too small to give this help, so find an older person who can.

Some Basic First Aid

Small Cuts and Scratches

Small cuts and scratches can become infected. They must be cared for in the right way. Here are four things you can do.

1. Wash the wound with soap and water.
2. Dry the skin.
3. Put bacteria-killing medicine on the wound.
4. Cover the wound with a bandage.

Bleeding Wounds

If the person is bleeding badly, you need to stop the bleeding.

1. Get a clean piece of cloth and put it on top of the wound. Do not remove the cloth.
2. Press carefully but firmly on the cloth.
3. Make sure the injury has no broken bones. Then lift and prop up the injured area to lessen the flow of blood.

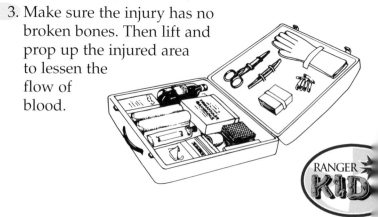

RANGER
KID

Minor Burns

Minor burns are fairly simple to treat.

1. Cool the burned area with cold water, not ice, for several minutes.
2. Carefully cover the skin with a dry bandage. Don't put any medical skin cream on a burn unless it is a very minor burn.

Insect Bites

Insect bites can be very itchy. An insect, like a bee, might leave a stinger in the skin.

1. Clean the area around the bite with soap and water.
2. Cover the area with a bandage.
3. For further relief, hold a cold pack on the area for several minutes.
4. If the victim develops a sudden rash or has a hard time breathing, call 911.

Rashes

Skin that has touched poison ivy or poison oak plants can become itchy. Sometimes you can prevent a rash.

Preventing a Rash

1. Rinse the skin in cool water to remove the oils that rub off the leaves.
2. Remove and wash your clothes as soon as possible after contact with the plants.

Treating a Rash

If you get a rash, follow these steps.

1. Try not to scratch the area. This may cause infection.
2. Put on calamine lotion to soothe the itching until the rash dries up.
3. If the rash is very severe, see a doctor.

Splinters

Small splinters should be removed from the skin as soon as they are noticed. Have an older friend or an adult help do the following.

1. Clean the area around the splinter with soap and water.
2. Clean a needle and tweezers with rubbing alcohol.
3. Use the needle to expose part of the splinter above the skin. Grasp the splinter firmly with the tweezers and gently pull it out of the skin.
4. Keep the wound clean and dry to prevent infection.

Blisters

Blisters form on your feet when your shoe (or boot) rubs your skin. Prevent blisters by wearing comfortable shoes that fit well. Wear socks that protect your skin from rub-

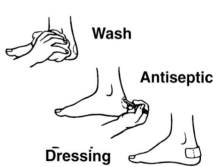

Wash

Antiseptic

Dressing

bing on the shoe. You may get a hot spot, a reddened area on your foot, before you get a blister. Put moleskin on it to protect it from further rubbing. Follow these steps if you get a blister.

1. If a blister forms, don't pop it. Let it go down by itself and it will heal.
2. If the blister has broken, clean it with soap and water, use a medical skin cream, and cover it with a bandage.

Puncture Wounds

Wounds caused by stepping or falling on nails or large splinters are called puncture wounds. The sharp object has punctured your skin. A doctor should treat all deep puncture wounds. These wounds can easily become infected. The victim may need a tetanus shot. Any puncture wound in the head, chest, or stomach needs to be looked at by a doctor.

Here's how to treat a minor puncture wound.

1. Soak the wound in hot soapy water for about 15 minutes.
2. Dry the wound.
3. Cover the wound with a bandage.

Be Ready; Be Safe

Learning to be safety-minded is not just smart. It is the Royal Rangers way. Remember the Royal Ranger Motto? Being ready for anything includes being ready for emergencies and disasters. Learn how to be of help during an emergency. Here are some tips.

Helping in Emergencies

When someone is injured and needs medical attention, you can help. Learn how to get medical assistance. It may save someone's life.

1. Know how to call authorities in an emergency. Dial 911 to report a medical emergency or a crime. If your county doesn't use 911, dial 0. An operator can connect you with the authorities for help. Or you can memorize the telephone numbers of the local police, fire, and ambulance services.

2. When you are with a friend and find someone who is hurt, here's what you do: The one who knows the most about helping an injured person stays and gives first aid. The other person goes for help. If you are by yourself, give the injured person first aid, then go for help.

Safety During Hunting Season

Royal Rangers activities should not be held where hunters may go during hunting season. Know the dates of hunting seasons in your area. During hunting seasons, hikes and camp-outs should be held in areas safe from hunters. Even if you are in an area that is off-limits to hunters, if it is hunting season—dress safely. Wear fluorescent orange. This color is not natural to fields and woods, so it is easily seen.

Distress Signals

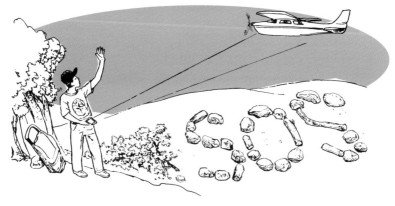

Being lost or unable to move outdoors may require a call for help, a distress signal. A common distress signal is a noise or a sign made three times—for example, three gunshots in the air, three blows of a whistle, three contained fires, or three columns of smoke.

A person can get the attention of a low-flying airplane in a number of ways: 1) putting a flag or blanket on a pole or tree; 2) using a mirror to reflect the sun into the sky; or 3) tramping an SOS in the snow, the sand, or a field. This is a common ground-to-air signal. (See picture.)

The Morse code distress call can be used. It can be made in a number of ways, for example, using a walkie-talkie, an air horn, or a flashlight. The distress call is three short, three long, and three short occurrences of sound or light.

Safe and Ready in the Home

Every Ranger's family should be prepared for emergencies. When a fire, flood, tornado, or other disaster hits a community, families suffer. A disaster that affects one person affects the rest of the family too. Everyone in a family can help. Talk about emergencies that could happen to your family or in your home. Be ready with a plan. Have on hand a well-equipped first aid kit for injuries.

You can also put together an emergency kit. Here are some items you might include:

1. Adequate non-spoilable food supply
2. Ample water supply
3. Rainwear
4. Flashlights
5. Battery-powered radios, with extra batteries
6. First aid supplies

An Emergency Plan for a Fire

Your home should have smoke detectors and fire extinguishers. They should be placed where they will be the most effective. Follow these suggested guidelines.

1. Place a smoke detector on each level of your house.

2. Place a fire extinguisher (preferably a 5–pound extinguisher) next to the kitchen and one near the furnace room. Can you find all the fire extinguishers in the picture on this page?

3. Smoke detectors and fire extinguishers should be checked regularly.

What is your family's escape plan in case of a fire? Fires make deadly gases that rise. So keep low to the floor as you escape. Fires create a black smoke, making it hard to see. Your family should practice the escape plan blindfolded or at night with all the lights out. Each family member should try to crawl from his or her bedroom to the nearest way out of the house. Think of two ways you could escape from your house; one way might be blocked by fire. What are at least two ways someone could get out of the house in the picture on this page?

If your house has an upstairs, have an escape ladder. Bedroom doors should be kept closed at night. This helps keep smoke and fire from moving from one room to the next.

An Emergency Plan for an Earthquake

An earthquake gives no warning. You must know what to do.

1. Stand in a doorway or get under something strong, like a table or desk.

2. Do not stand or sit near a window, loose objects on a shelf, or a heating unit.

3. Once the earthquake is over, ask an adult if the utilities, water, gas and electricity, need to be turned off. An earthquake can break water pipes and gas lines.

An Emergency Plan for a Tornado

A tornado can drop out of the sky in seconds. Tornadoes produce winds of more than 200 miles an hour. Most people injured by tornadoes are hurt by the things that fly through the air during a tornado. Know the weather that brings tornadoes and what to do when one appears.

1. Move quickly to a safe location, such as a hallway or basement.

2. Stay away from windows. A window can explode because of the sudden change in the air pressure. (Do not waste time trying to open windows.)

3. On the ground level, move to a bathroom, a closet, an inner hallway, or underneath a stairway.

4. If possible, cover yourself with a bed mattress.

5. People living in a mobile home should find other shelter in a school, church or building with a basement.

6. People in a vehicle should do the same as if they were in a mobile home.

7. Stay in a safe area until the storm passes and the all-clear signal is given.

An Emergency Plan for a Flood

Heavy rains often cause flooding on low ground. The rain fills gullies and ravines with rushing water, often without warning. These are called flash floods. People caught in flash floods can drown. Do not try to act brave by staying in a dangerous area. If a flood occurs in your area, go to higher ground. If you are with others, stay with them.

An Emergency Plan for a Hurricane

Hurricanes are storms that begin out on the ocean and move onto land. The wind of a hurricane blows seventy-four miles an hour or more. A hurricane causes flooding and water damage. It can blow down small buildings. The U.S. Weather Bureau watches ocean storms. They report how strong they are and where they are moving. Sometimes people have several hours to get ready. They board up their windows and buy extra food. Local authorities will tell you if your house is in danger. Your parents will know what to do.

Chapter 7
You and the Bible

101

The Bible

I carry my Bible with me everywhere I go. See it in my hand? Do you have your own Bible? God's Word is filled with adventure and excitement. The Bible tells the story of God and His plan for people. Everyone around the world can be saved by believing in Jesus. The following stories will tell you more about the Bible. Have someone read these pages with you. Ask your mom, dad or grandparent to read to you.

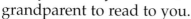

The Bible is really 66 books, like a small library. The books were written over a long time, 1600 years. More than 35 men wrote these books. God spoke to each man. He told them about himself. He said He was the only God and that He had made everything.

God also told the writers of the Bible how He wants people to live. For example, He gave the Ten Commandments. In the Bible, we also read about God's great love. The world was disobeying God. So He sent His Son, Jesus, to save people from their sin. Then they could start over and obey Him. All they had to do was believe that Jesus was God's Son, their Savior.

Here are some important Bible stories. Read them. God is as great and as good today as He was in Bible times. What He did for people then, He can do for you.

God the Creator
(Genesis 1:1 to 2:3)

Have you ever wondered where you came from? Who were the first man and first woman? How did they get here? The Bible answers those questions. The Bible begins with the Book of Genesis. The Book of Genesis begins, "In the beginning…." Some of the "beginnings" we learn about are how the world began and how people began. So Genesis is called the Book of Beginnings.

The first verse in the Bible says, "In the beginning God created the sky and the earth." The Bible tells us that the earth was empty and had no form. The ocean was covered with darkness. The Bible also tells us that God's Spirit was moving over the ocean.

Then God spoke. God is so powerful He can make something happen just by speaking. "Let there be light!" He said. And what happened? There was light. So the darkness passed, and the morning came. This made the first day.

The second day God spoke again. He caused air to separate the waters. Now there was sky and water.

The third day God caused the waters to come together. Land was uncovered. Then God said, "Let the earth produce plants." And it did.

Grass and trees grew all over the earth. Still, no sun, moon, or stars were seen.

On the fourth day God commanded lights to appear in the sky: a bright light for the day and a soft light for the night. The bright light was the sun; the soft light was the moon. God put stars in the sky, too.

The next day, the fifth day, God created birds to fly in the air and fish to swim in the water. "Let the water be filled with living things. And let birds fly in the air above the earth," He said. So all kinds of living creatures were created to live in the rivers and seas. Many birds filled the air.

On the sixth day God made every kind of animal, big and little, wild and tame. He made turtles and elephants, cats and kangaroos, horses and monkeys. What variety God created! But God was not through. It was time for His greatest creation—human beings. God said, "Let us make human beings in our image and likeness. And let them rule." So God created Adam and Eve, a man and a woman. He made them "in His image." That means He made them knowing right from wrong. He gave them a conscience. He also gave them special abil-

RANGER KID

ities: the abilities to know Him, to love Him, and to choose Him. He gave them the power of choice. They could choose good or bad, right or wrong. They could decide whether they would love and serve Him.

On the seventh day God rested. He was not tired. He just thought it was a good idea. He had finished creating. Everything God created was great. But His greatest creation was not the earth. It was not mountains or rivers or forests. God's greatest creation was not the wondrous animals on the earth. God's greatest creation was us, human beings. He sent His Son for people. He can bring light and life to a heart full of darkness. He just says, "I forgive you." Have you let Him forgive you?

The Birth of Jesus
(Luke 2:1–20)

The emperor of Rome had said that everyone had to be counted. He told everyone to go home, to the place where they had been born. That's where they would

be counted. So people from all over the little land of Palestine were on the move. They were going back to the places of their birth. The roads to the village of Bethlehem were filled with travelers.

Mary and Joseph were among these travelers. They had been walking a long way. They were tired, especially Mary. She was going to have a baby very soon. Mary and Joseph were glad they were close to Bethlehem. They were eager to find a place to stay for the night. They need-ed to rest.

But the town was crowded. Joseph looked for an inn (like a motel) where they could stay. He looked and looked, but every place was full. Finally an innkeeper said they could sleep in his stable with the animals.

They were thankful to God; they had found a place to rest. Then, during the night a wonderful thing happened: Mary had her baby. God's only Son had come to earth. An angel had told Joseph to name the baby Jesus. This

RANGER KID

was very important. Jesus means "the Lord saves." God's Son had come to save all people from their sins.

Mary wrapped baby Jesus in cloths. Then she laid Him in the feedbox for the stable animals.

That same night, shepherds were watching their sheep in the fields near Bethlehem. Suddenly, a bright light shone around them and an angel appeared. This frightened the shepherds. "Don't be afraid," said the angel. "I am bringing you some good news. It will be a joy to all the people. Today your Savior was born in David's town. He is Christ, the Lord. This is how you will know him: You will find a baby wrapped in cloths and lying in a feeding box." Then the sky was filled with angels. They began praising God and saying, "Give glory to God in heaven, and on earth let there be peace to the people who please God." Then, just as suddenly as the angels had come, they went back to heaven.

The shepherds talked about this great news. "Let us go to Bethlehem and see this," they said. So they hurried to Bethlehem. There they found the baby Jesus lying in a feeding box. He was wrapped just the way the angel had said. There was no doubt about it. This baby was God's only Son.

The shepherds started back to their sheep. They praised and thanked God for what they had heard and seen. They probably told everyone they met about the angels and the baby. Their Savior, the Messiah, had been born! They had seen Him! We also can thank and praise God for sending His Son Jesus to us. He is our Savior too.

Victory Over Temptation
(Matthew 4:1–11)

If only I can make Jesus sin! the devil probably thought. He knew that Jesus could not be the Savior if He sinned. Then He would not be the perfect Savior who could take away sin. So for more than a month the devil tempted Jesus. Again and again the devil tried to get Jesus to do wrong.

During that time of being tempted, Jesus did not eat. He was praying and thinking about God. For more than a month, Jesus didn't even eat bread. He became very hungry.

The devil knew that Jesus was hungry, that Jesus was weak. *Now is my chance to trick Him!* the devil thought.

"If you are the Son of God, tell these rocks to become bread," the devil said.

Jesus could have made bread

out of rocks. He is God and He can do anything. But Jesus knew He was not to use His power just to please himself. He would use His power the way His Father in heaven would want Him to. So Jesus controlled His hunger. He said "no" to the devil's suggestion. Jesus wouldn't turn rocks into bread just because He was hungry.

"It is written in the Scriptures: 'A person does not live only by eating bread. But a person lives by everything the Lord says,' " Jesus said to the devil. Jesus knew God's Word and told the devil what it said. The devil had nothing more to say then.

Jesus had stopped the devil by quoting the Scripture. But the devil came to tempt Jesus again. And this time the devil quoted God's Word! (Remember that the devil can quote the Bible.) He took Jesus to Jerusalem and put Him on a high part of the temple. Then the devil said to Jesus, "If you are the Son of God, jump off. It is written in the Scriptures, 'He has put his angels in charge of you. They will catch you with their hands. And you will not hit your foot on a rock.' "

That was true. Angels would take care of Jesus after the devil went away and an angel would take care of Him just before He went to the cross. But jumping off the temple now would be just showing off. Besides, Jesus knew all of God's Word, not just a little of it. So He said, "It also says in the Scriptures: 'Do not test the Lord your God.' "

Jesus said "no" to showing off how special He was. The devil had to try something else. This time he took Jesus to a high mountain. From there the devil showed Jesus all the kingdoms in the world and all the great things in them. "If you will bow down and worship me, I will give you all these things," said the devil.

"Go away from me, Satan!" Jesus commanded. Again He quoted God's Word: "It is written in the Scriptures, 'You must worship the Lord your God. Serve only Him!'" Jesus had won the battle with the devil. He had said "no" to what the devil wanted Him to do. This had been a hard test for Jesus. So God sent angels to care for Jesus.

Jesus had been tempted by the devil three times. But Jesus was a strong fighter against the devil. Three times He had said "no"; He would not do what the devil wanted. He was going to do what God wanted. He would say "yes" to God. He would go to the Cross to die for the sins of the world. He would be the perfect Savior.

The devil still tempts people today. He tells them they can be rich. They can be powerful. All they have to do is what the devil wants. Jesus beat the devil, and He can help us beat the devil. Jesus knows about the devil's tricks. God's Word helped Jesus say "no" to the devil and "yes" to God. It can help us say "no" to the devil and "yes" to God. We must learn what the Bible says. We must remember to ask for Jesus' help. He will help us.

Jesus Teaches About Salvation
(John 3:1–21)

Nicodemus was an important Jewish leader. He was a teacher among the Jews in Jerusalem. He had heard of Jesus. He wanted to know more about what Jesus taught. One night he went to the house where Jesus was.

"Teacher," he said, "we know that you are a teacher sent from God. No one can do the miracles you do, unless God is with him." Jesus could tell what Nicodemus wanted. Nicodemus wanted to find out how to become a part of God's kingdom.

Jesus said, "I tell you the truth. Unless one is born again, he cannot be in God's kingdom."

Nicodemus was puzzled. He did not understand what Jesus meant. Nicodemus asked

how a grownup could become a baby again. Jesus explained that He was talking about a person's spirit. The spirit in a person needs to be brought to life by God's power.

Jesus went on to say, "For God loved the world so much that he gave his only Son. God gave his Son so that whoever believes in him may not be lost, but have eternal life."

Jesus knew that everyone has sinned. Nicodemus was a religious man. But he still needed God to forgive his sins. We are sinners too. We must be sorry for our sins and ask God to forgive us. When God forgives us, He makes us new. Our spirits come to life. We call this being born again. We join God's kingdom; we become members of His family.

Have you ever asked Jesus to forgive you? If not, do it right now. Stop and pray. Say, "Jesus, forgive me of my sins. Come make me a new person. I want to be born again. Amen." Now be sure to tell your commander and parents.

RANGER
KID

Jesus Heals a Boy
(John 4:46–53)

In Capernaum, a town in the country of Galilee, there lived a rich man. He was an important official in the king's court. But he was sad. His son was very, very sick.

Then he heard that Jesus was in Galilee. Jesus had been in Jerusalem and had healed people. The news of His miracles was talked about everywhere, even in Capernaum. Now He had returned to the town of Cana, another town in Galilee. Once Jesus had attended a wedding in Cana. He had even done a miracle there. Now He was back. The royal official was sure Jesus could heal his son.

"I'll go to Cana and ask Jesus to come here to Capernaum. He can make my boy well," the official

decided. He set out for Cana as fast as he could. It was a two-day journey. His boy was now sick enough to die.

At last the worried father arrived in Cana. He hurried to Jesus. "Jesus, please come to Capernaum. My boy is very, very sick," he said. "He is about to die."

Jesus said simply, "Go. Your son will live." The official turned and started home. He believed that Jesus had healed his son without seeing him.

The next day the man was nearing his home. He saw some people coming toward him. They were his servants bringing him good news: "Your son is well!"

The man asked, "What time did my son begin to get well?"

They answered, "It was about one o'clock yesterday when the fever left him."

The boy was healed at the exact time Jesus had said "Your son will live." The father was happy, of course. So was the rest of the family. He had believed Jesus could heal his son. Now he believed Jesus was God's Son. He was ready to trust Jesus, to follow Him, and to serve Him. Today, Jesus is still healing people who believe in Him. If you need to be healed, pray and ask Jesus to heal you.

Jesus Stops Storms
(Matthew 8:23–27; Mark 4:35–41;
Luke 8:22–25)

Jesus had been teaching people all day long. At the end of the day He was very, very tired.

"Come with me across the lake," Jesus said to His disciples. They all got into a boat and sailed away. Jesus lay down in the bottom of the boat and went to sleep.

While Jesus was sleeping, a cool wind began to

blow. The wind blew in clouds from the mountains. The clouds grew dark and the wind became cold. The blowing wind rippled across the water. Small waves became big waves. Soon the whole lake was dark and rolling. The boat was rocking. Waves splashed into the boat. The disciples were worried. Then they were afraid. Jesus was still asleep.

This storm is going to turn over our boat. We will drown, they thought. They wished Jesus were awake. Jesus would know what to do. How could He sleep in such a storm! The disciples wanted Jesus to know that they were all in danger. They went to Jesus and woke Him up.

"Teacher do you care about us?" they asked. "We will drown!"

Jesus stood up and looked around. He gave a command to the lake—"Quiet! Be still!"

The wind stopped blowing. The waves stopped rolling. The water grew calm and still. The lake was peaceful again. And the disciples were amazed. They had seen Jesus heal the sick. They knew He had power over disease. Now they knew He had power over nature too. Even the winds and the waves obeyed Him.

Jesus has all power. We may get sick but Jesus can heal us. We may be in a storm but Jesus can stop the storm. He can take away our fear. Jesus can help us today just like He helped His disciples. We must learn to trust Him.

RANGER
KID

Jesus Teaches How to Pray

(Matthew 6:9–13; Luke 11:1–10)

Jesus had just finished praying. His disciples came to Him and said, "Lord, teach us how to pray." They wanted to be like Jesus. They wanted to talk to God like Jesus did.

So Jesus gave them a prayer to follow. Often it is called the Lord's Prayer. It could be called a Disciple's Prayer. We can use it to learn how to pray.

The prayer begins "Our Father in heaven." There are many fathers on earth. But in heaven there is only one Father. He is a Father to all who believe in His Son. He is the best Father. Every father on earth should be like Him. We can come to our heavenly Father like a small child comes to a good earthly father. And we can talk to our Father in heaven. Prayer is just talking to God like talking to a father who loves us.

Jesus taught that prayer should put God first. Jesus began by saying "Our father." Then He said, "We pray that your name will always be kept holy." Prayer should begin by honoring God.

Then Jesus said, "We pray that your kingdom will come." We make God our King now. Then one day He will bring His kingdom. We will be ready, because we have already made Him our King and we have been praying for His kingdom to come.

"We pray that what you want will be done, here on earth as it is in heaven." Heaven is the best place there is: No lying, no fighting, no bullies, no tears or good-byes. Heaven is all joy, all goodness, and all love. Everyone in heaven obeys God. That makes good things happen. If everyone obeyed God on earth, if everyone did God's will, that would make earth like heaven.

Prayer is also a time to ask for help. It is a time to ask for things we need. Our Father in heaven knows how to take care of us.

Prayer is our time to ask for forgiveness. We do wrong. We don't take up for someone. Or we say mean things. We are not acting like God's children. That makes us feel bad. It makes others feel bad. Our heavenly Father feels bad too. We need to ask for forgiveness. We need to say we're sorry. Prayer helps us do that.

God can keep us from doing wrong when we are tempted. We need God's help. The devil is stronger than we are. We cannot say "no" to him by ourselves. So Jesus teaches us to pray for help from our Father in heaven.

RANGER KID

Why Jesus Died
(Luke 23:1–23; John 18:28 to 19:37)

A crowd gathered outside Pilate's judgment hall. They wanted Pilate, the governor, to sentence Jesus to death.

"What is his crime?" Pilate asked.

The people couldn't name a real crime that Jesus had done. They were jealous of Jesus. The Jewish leaders didn't want the people to follow Him. They wanted Jesus dead. So they made up things about Him. Pilate could see that.

"He hasn't done anything," Pilate told them. "He has too," they said. Pilate said, "Then you take him and judge him." The Jews were angry and said, "We don't have the right to put anyone to death." If Pilate did not do what the Jewish leaders wanted, they might riot. The emperor in Rome would think Pilate was not a good leader.

Pilate went inside the judgment hall and asked Jesus, "Are you the king of the Jews?" Jesus said He was a king but His kingdom was not on earth. Pilate went back to the crowd.

"You have a custom that a prisoner be freed at this time of year," Pilate told the people. "Who shall it be? Jesus or Barabbas?" (Barabbas was a robber.) Pilate wanted the people to say, "Release Jesus." But they wanted the robber to go free.

Pilate tried one more time to get the Jews to choose Jesus. He had Jesus whipped. Then he showed Him to the crowd. He hoped they would think Jesus had been punished enough.

But the crowd was not listening to Pilate. They were listening to the chief priests and elders. They were shouting, "Kill him on a cross!"

"Why?" asked Pilate. "I can find no reason to kill him."

"He said he was the Son of God," they answered. "Our Law says he should die for saying that."

Pilate became very scared. He did not know who Jesus was. He did not like to think that He might be someone very special. "Who are you? Where are you from?" Pilate asked. "I have the power to set you free and the power to have you killed." But Jesus told Pilate: "The only power you have is the power God gave you." Now Pilate really wanted to set Jesus free.

"Kill him on a cross!" the crowd yelled again. "If you let Jesus go, you aren't the emperor's friend." Pilate wanted to be the emperor's friend. He wanted to be the governor of the Jews. So he ordered Jesus to be killed on a cross.

God allowed His Son to die. Do you know why? Because sin had separated people from God and Jesus was on a mission to bring God and people back together. He took all people's sins as if they were His own. He was our sin offering on the Cross. He died for everything about people that is wrong—selfishness, bad tempers, jealousy, lying. Anyone who wants to can now come back to God. We can be friends with God again.

Jesus, the Risen Lord
(Matthew 27:57 to 28:15)

Jesus had been put to death. A rich man named Joseph went to Pilate and asked permission to take care of Jesus' body. Joseph owned a tomb carved in rock, like a cave. He put Jesus' body there. Then he rolled a big round flat stone in front of it. The stone had been carved to seal the tomb.

Jesus had said He would come back to life. His followers had forgotten this. The priests and elders, the leaders of the Jews, hadn't forgotten this. They just didn't believe it. They told Pilate that Jesus' followers might steal His body. Then His followers might pretend that Jesus had come back to life. So the leaders of the Jews asked Pilate for soldiers to guard the tomb.

So Roman soldiers were sent to guard the tomb. But early on Sunday morning there was an earthquake. An angel of the Lord came and rolled away the big stone in front of the tomb. The angel was as bright as lightning. His clothes were as white as snow. The guards went into shock. They could see what was happening, but they could not move.

Afterwards, two women, Mary and Mary Magdalene, came to the tomb. They saw that the stone had been rolled aside and an angel was sitting on it! "Don't be afraid," said the angel. "You are looking for Jesus, who was killed on the cross. He is not here. He came back to life! Look inside the tomb. Go and tell His disciples. Jesus is going to meet them in Galilee just like He said He would." The women left the tomb quickly. They went to tell the disciples the great news.

The women hurried away. Jesus was alive! They wanted to tell the things they had seen and heard. Then they got a great surprise. Jesus himself met them.

"Hello," said Jesus.

The women knelt and worshiped Him.

"Don't be afraid," said Jesus. "Go and tell my brothers to go on to Galilee. They will see me there."

Meanwhile, the guards had come out of shock. They went and reported to the Jewish priests what had happened. The priests became upset. They did not care that Jesus really had come back to life. They didn't want anybody to know. So they paid the soldiers to lie about what had happened.

"We want you to say, 'His disciples came during the night. They stole his body while we were sleeping.' If the governor hears this report, we will pay him off. That will keep you out of trouble."

The soldiers took the money and told the story. But lies don't change the truth. Jesus had come back from the dead and He is alive forever. Because Jesus lives, His Spirit can be with us all the time. Because God brought Jesus to life, He can bring us to life too.

The Coming of the Holy Spirit

(Acts 1:4 to 2:41)

After Jesus came back to life, He stayed with His followers for more than a month. Once when He was eating with them, He told them not leave Jerusalem. He said, "The Father has made you a promise which I told you about before. Wait here to receive this promise. The Holy Spirit will come to you. Then you will receive power. You will be my witnesses—in Jerusalem, in all of Judea, in Samaria, and in every part of the world." (Acts 1:4,8). The disciples were obedient. They did not go back to Galilee. They found a place to stay in Jerusalem. Then they waited for the Holy Spirit Jesus had promised to send.

About ten days later, a sound filled the house where Jesus' followers were. It sounded like a strong wind. They saw something that looked like fiery tongues. A fiery tongue appeared over each person in the room. Then something else happened: All these Jews from Galilee began to speak languages they had never learned. Each person

began speaking a language that was spoken in another country.

It was a special time of year for Jews. They came for a special celebration—Pentecost—in Jerusalem. Jews from many faraway countries had come. Now they heard their countries' languages spoken. They moved closer to see what was happening. They saw people who were not from their country speaking their language.

"Aren't all these people from Galilee?" they asked. They wondered how they could speak their languages. They were very puzzled. God was being praised in their own languages. The languages were being spoken by Jews from Galilee. They did not know that these were followers of Jesus.

Many of the Jews were amazed. But others made fun of the Galileans. "These people are drunk," they said.

Then Peter began to preach. He stepped out in front of the crowd and began to speak to them in his own language. He said the prophet Joel had talked about what was happening—more than 800 years earlier. God had said, "I will give my Spirit freely to all kinds of people. Your sons and daughters will prophesy. Your old men will dream dreams. Your young men will see visions. At that time I will give my Spirit even to my servants, both men and women. And they will prophesy" (Acts 2:17,18).

"This is what was spoken by the prophet Joel," Peter told them.

Then Peter went on to say that this outpouring of the Spirit was for everyone, not just Jews. "The promise," Peter said, "is for you and your children and for all who are far off—for all whom the Lord our God will call." That promise includes you and me.

Today God still sends His Spirit from heaven just as He did that day in Jerusalem. The promise of His Spirit is still good. People are baptized in the Holy Spirit today. The Holy Spirit still gives them a language they never learned. Speaking in a language you have never learned shows that you have been filled with the Holy Spirit.

In the Bible the Holy Spirit has different names. One of His names is the Helper. Jesus promised to send someone in His place: "I will ask the Father, and he will give you another Helper. He will give you this Helper to be with you forever" (John 14:16). Here are some of the ways the Holy Spirit helps us:

1. He wants to help us tell others about Jesus.

At Jesus' trial, Peter was afraid to say he knew Jesus. After Jesus went to heaven, He sent back His Spirit to Peter and other believers on the Day of Pentecost. Then Peter was not afraid to tell thousands of people about Jesus. God's Spirit will give us courage to tell others about Jesus too.

2. He wants to help us understand the Bible.

The Holy Spirit helped Peter understand the prophet Joel. Peter preached that God was going to give His Spirit to all kinds of people. The Holy Spirit can help us to understand God's Word better too.

3. He will help us to know Jesus better.

Jesus said, "The Spirit of truth [another name for the Holy Spirit] will bring glory to me. He will take what I have to say and tell it to you" (John 16:14). We can know Jesus better because of the Holy Spirit.

4. He will help us bring others to meet Jesus.

Peter preached to the crowd about Jesus being killed on a cross. Many people asked, "What shall we do?" "Ask God for forgiveness," was the answer. That very day 3,000 people believed that Jesus was their Savior. The Holy Spirit will help us tell others Jesus will forgive them.

5. He will help us when we are hurt and afraid.

One day Peter was put in jail because he talked about Jesus. Then he was beaten. But when they let him out, he said he would do what God wanted, not what people wanted. He was happy to be put in jail for Jesus.

Aren't you glad God sends the Helper to us? Talk to your commander or your mom or dad about the Holy Spirit. Tell them you want to be baptized in the Spirit. The Holy Spirit is a gift God promised us. Tell God you would like His Spirit to be your Helper.

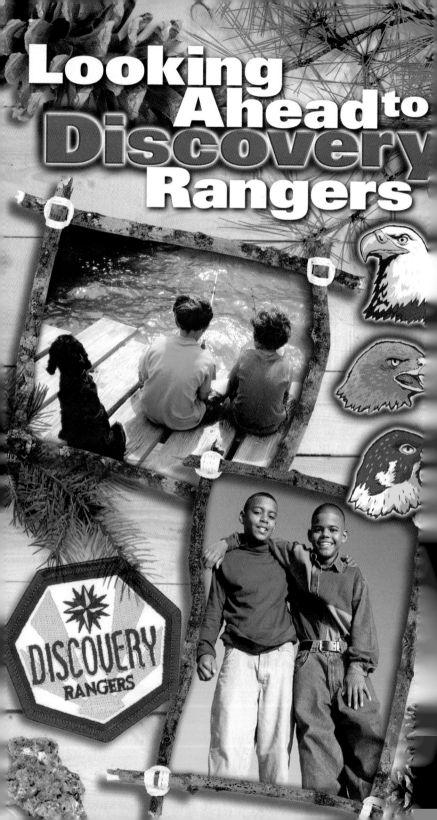

Looking Ahead to Discovery Rangers